MARY MASHUTA

Cotton Candy Quilts

USING FEED SACKS, VINTAGE & REPRODUCTION FABRICS

C&T PUBLISHING

dedication

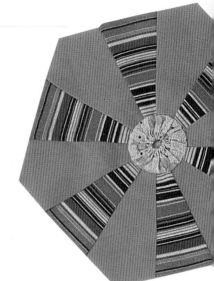

*This book is dedicated to two women who
never met:*

My maternal grandmother, George
McLeod Peterson, who provided my
link with America's quilting past.

Susan Dague, who had the good sense
to start collecting mid-twentieth-century
quilt tops and fabrics in the 1980s, and
who generously shared her time, quilts,
and fabrics with me.

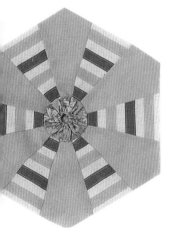

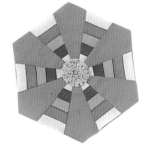

©2001 Mary Mashuta
Illustrations ©2001 C&T Publishing

Front Cover: *Circle Within Circle* by Mary Mashuta
Back Cover: *Grandmother's Gift* by Gay Nichols

Editor: Liz Aneloski
Technical Editors: Lynn Koolish and Catherine Comyns
Copy Editor: Carol Barrett
Design Director: Diane Pedersen
Production Assistant: Stephanie Muir
Book Designer: Rose Sheifer
Quilt Photographer: Sharon Risedorph
Illustrator: Richard Sheppard

Published by C&T Publishing, Inc. P.O. Box 1456, Lafayette, California 94549

Attention Teachers:
C&T Publishing, Inc. encourages you to use this book as a text for teaching. Contact us at 800-284-1114 or www.ctpub.com for more
information about the C&T Teachers Program.

We take great care to ensure that the information included in this book is accurate and presented in good faith, but no warranty is
provided nor results guaranteed. Since we have no control over the choice of materials or procedures used, neither the author nor C&T
Publishing, Inc. shall have any liability to any person or entity with respect to any loss or damage caused directly or indirectly by the
information contained in this book.

Trademarked (™) and Registered Trademarked (®) names are used throughout this book. Rather than use the symbols with every
occurrence of a trademark and registered trademark name, we are using the names only in an editorial fashion and to the benefit of the
owner, with no intention of infringement.

Library of Congress Cataloging-in-Publication Data

Mashuta, Mary.
  Cotton candy quilts : using feed sacks, vintage and reproduction fabrics / Mary Mashuta.
    p. cm.
Includes index.
  ISBN 1-57120-153-X
1. Patchwork--Patterns. 2. Patchwork quilts--United
States--History--20th century. 3. Textile fabrics--Reproduction. 4. Bagging. I. Title.
  TT835 .M27365 2001
  746.46'041--dc21   00-011627

Printed in China

10 9 8 7 6 5 4 3 2

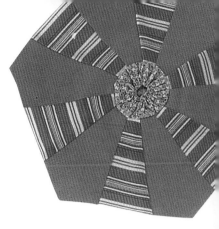

Contents

Introduction

Some time ago I became interested in the fabric and quilt patterns from mid-twentieth-century quilts (1920s to the beginning of the quilt revival of the 1970s). As I studied these fabrics and quilts, I tried replicating some of the quilts, but was also eager to discover new directions I could take by adding fabrics that weren't available at that time. My grandmother would certainly have enjoyed some of the fabrics I have at my disposal today. I wonder what she would have done with them? When I decided to write a book I wanted to look at the quilts of this particular era, not just as a historian, but as a contemporary quiltmaker looking to bring new insights to my work.

Some of us who made quilts for this book endeavored to reproduce the quilts that inspired us. The process made us look closely at what we were trying to copy. It raised questions of why things were done a certain way, and helped us to analyze why things did or didn't work. It also helped us gain a feeling for the sensitivity of the design period and made us more knowledgeable about the fabrics of this time period. Using this information, we could avoid some of the most common deviations, such as using white-on-white printed fabrics as a muslin substitute and including stipple machine quilting, in order to create our reproductions as accurately as possible.

This understanding was necessary as we made the decision whether to make a true-to-the-era replica of a vintage quilt, or merely to use the vintage quilt for inspiration, as the maker endeavored to make the quilt her own (which I often encouraged). However, it is important to be aware that there was a deviation from creating an accurate replica and know that this was a conscious decision.

It is also important to keep in mind that there are three viewing distances: the "across-a-crowded-room" distance; the "four-to-eight-feet, aisle-viewing" distance; and the "up-close-and-personal" distance. Each viewing distance tells something different about a quilt. One that looks old when viewed from across the room might be obviously new when inspected up close.

Join me now, as we study quilts made with fabric from the "near past." This book is about savoring the past, but it is also about the present.

Let me end with an analogy.

My sister and I have a set of twentieth-century Fiesta dishes. The "mix and match the colors" feature is one of the main reasons that Fiesta dishes are as popular today as they were when I was young. Half the fun of owning the bright, pastel dishes is that you get to constantly create new color combinations as the table is set. There are only two table setting rules at our house: the first is that each place setting must be multicolored, and the second is that no setting can match any other setting at the table.

Fiesta dishes: No one-color place settings allowed.

Fiesta dishes and French Provincial linens

Fiesta dishes, denim woven place mat, and Ralph Lauren™ napkin

Fiesta dishes and block printed linens from India

One of my real pleasures is to find new linens that can be combined with my Fiesta dishes. I can choose linens that have a "time-appropriate" look, to give a nostalgic feeling (like making a reproduction quilt), or choose linens that have an updated look, to give a fresh, new feeling (like making a quilt using an old quilt for inspiration). This allows me to continue the enjoyment of my wonderful dishes.

Art is not static. It is constantly changing. New thoughts, processes, and products are added as time passes. Please keep this in mind as you read through my book.

Fiesta dishes and Hawaiian linens

About the Fabric

CHAPTER 1

Three events started me on the path to creating this book:

● The purchase of my first reproduction, twentieth-century fabrics in a quilt store named Hearts and Hands in Tokyo, Japan in 1986.

● The gift in 1990 from Sonya Barrington of two paper bags filled with her grandmother Mabel Hartman Combs's scraps.

● The purchase of my first feed sack squares while I was teaching at the 22nd National Quilting Association Show in Lincoln, Nebraska in 1991.

Over the years more fabric was added to my stash, and eventually I began making quilts from it.

What is this fabric called besides twentieth-century fabric? Actually, there are two major groups as I see it—the "real stuff" (which includes feed sacks and vintage fabrics) and the reproduction fabrics. All of these can be used for the projects in this book. The first group is truly old. The second group is comprised of new fabrics that have been designed to look like the old fabrics they are mimicking. Let's explore these wonderful fabrics further.

Fabrics designed by Sanki Nohara.

Feed sacks with paper labels. Collection of author.

feed sacks

Feed sacks, or utility bags, came into use after the Civil War and were popular through the 1950s. At first the bags were commercially produced as plain bags, but the American entrepreneurial spirit soon took over and brand names and advertising were printed on the sacks. It was difficult to remove the printing if you wanted to recycle the bags, so eventually paper labels were substituted. Somewhere along the way, manufacturers began printing designs on the bags. This was an enormous success and promoted brand loyalty. Companies employed their own designers and a tremendous number of patterns were created over the years. Some bags are still manufactured today.

Most people think of feed sacks and the Great Depression when they think of old fabrics from the twentieth century. Many of us have heard tales of dresses and household items that were made from feed sacks. (It took three or four large, matching feed sacks to make a dress.) The romance of the feed sack is part of the collective American past and present … getting something for nothing. The added bonus was that you ended up with something that was also useful. For many, thriftiness was a way of life out of necessity. Frugalness was to be admired.

Printed feed sack. Collection Susan Dague, Piedmont, California.

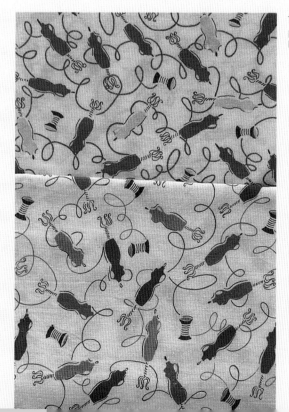

Two colorways of feed sack print. Collection of Susan Dague, Piedmont, California.

Feed sack corners. Collection of author.

vintage fabrics

Sometimes we get so caught up in the "romance of the feed sack" that we forget that it was possible to buy fabric yardage in stores. The operative phrase here is "buy"—it had to be paid for. This was the kind of fabric that came to me from Sonya Barrington as Mabel's scraps (page 6). It was sold by the yard in stores and by mail order.

Today this is categorized as "vintage" fabric. (Even though feed sacks are vintage, they are a recognized category.) We could even borrow a term from the auto industry and call it "previously owned." The word "vintage" has class, but can be intimidating. It makes us realize that it is scarce, probably costs a fair amount, and most likely can't be replaced if we don't do it right the first time. All of a sudden, old has class.

Ann Rhode with her Aunt Aravilla

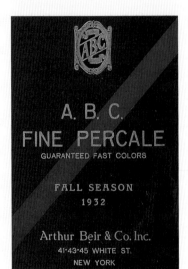

A.B.C. Fine Percale. Fall Season, 1932. Collection of Nancyann J. Twelker, Shoreline, Washington.

Page from A.B.C. Fine Percale book. Collection of Nancyann J. Twelker, Shoreline, Washington.

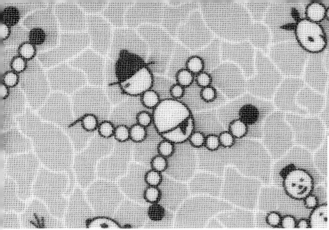

Vintage (left) and modern reproduction by Sharon Newman (right)

reproduction fabrics

Reproduction fabrics are produced today using vintage fabric as the design source and are readily available. Recently we have seen '50s and '70s collections added to those of the '20s, '30s, and '40s. Some of my students have huge stashes of reproduction fabrics. (A goodly number have yet to cut into them when they tote them to class!)

finding fabrics

Feed sacks and vintage fabrics can be found at quilt shows and at garage and estate sales. They can also be mail ordered and purchased over the Internet. Vintage fabric may even be in your own closet.

Over the years the feed sacks can collect spores, mildew, and dust, and smell terrible. Wash them using Vintage Soak to remove spots and stains. Smaller scraps can be hand-basted together in little piles and placed in lingerie bags. If the stains don't come out, you can still use the fabric. (Like us, it takes years to collect spots and stains, why not savor them as a badge of age?)

learning about history

The newly-made quilts in this book were inspired by many things—vintage quilts and tops, vintage and new blocks, vintage and reproduction fabrics, and yoyos, rick rack, and buttons that would have been used in the time period (although not necessarily on quilts). Along the way, I learned more about what living in America used to be like from simple stories that quilters have shared with me about their lives and families.

so now what ...

I find that many people are attracted to one or the other of our basic fabric groups—the "real" fabrics or the reproduction fabrics, but usually not both. The two groups of quilters seem to be exclusive of each other. In the end, however, the fabrics have much in common and can be studied together as far as design is concerned. I have included both old and new fabrics. For this reason many of the examples are presented in more than one version. Some have been constructed with feed sacks and/or vintage fabrics; others, with reproduction fabrics.

Cotton Candy Deluxe Lollipop©. Collection of Roberta Horton, Berkeley, California.

Characteristics

Following are some of the characteristics that are found in mid-twentieth-century quilts (1920s to the beginning of the quilt revival of the 1970s). As quilting has evolved over the years, so have many of the methods and techniques we use. Even if you use traditional blocks in your quilts, you probably use some of these modern methods such as rotary cutting and machine piecing, appliqué, and quilting. We don't even use fabric in the same way earlier quilters did.

fabric

Fabric tells us a lot about a quilt. It gives us clues about when the quilt was made. Most of the quilts I discuss in this book are scrap quilts, so they contain many different fabrics, usually collected over a span of years.

Color

Color changes with the times. Every year new fashion colors are introduced. When the new colors are first introduced they are shocking. If the colors are accepted we become accustomed to seeing, wearing, and using them. Eventually we crave something new, so these colors go out of fashion. Fabric colors evolved from the "murky" colors of the Victorian era to the pastels of the 1920s. Houses became cleaner, women were more liberated after WW I, and new dyes were invented. Women were ready for these pretty pastels which took a lot less dye to produce during these times when frugality was the rule.

Colors became brighter in the 1930s. Color names like Nile Green, Mint Green, Bubblegum Pink, and Tangerine were introduced. Blues became darker. More multicolor prints were available, and they became busier and more colorful through the 1940s.

The 1950s gave us pink in combination with gray or blue. Turquoise was another hot color. "Modern" prints became available.

The pink changed to hot pink in the 1960s and was often combined with chartreuse green. Avocado green and orange were another winning combination.

By the time the quilt revival came around in the 1970s we were back to murky colors! Those of us who became quilters at that time shudder when we see those old calicos we so dearly loved.

Using Solids

Most people think "busy prints" when they think about mid-twentieth-century quilts, but believe it or not, solid-colored fabrics played an important part in the quilts we will be studying.

Lack of detail in solid fabrics acts as a calming element for busy prints. These plain areas give the eye a place to rest. Muslin was very popular for backgrounds because it was cheap, plain, and safe. I gravitate to the colored solids of the time period. They can be used for pieced and appliquéd blocks that require a background (negative space).

Adding a contemporary note, some of us have substituted hand-dyed fabrics and hand-dyed-look-alikes rather than solid colors in our quilts. They are a dead giveaway that our quilts are not old, but I think they breathe new life into them. (For example, see page 44.)

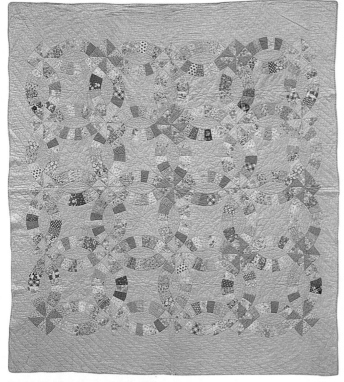

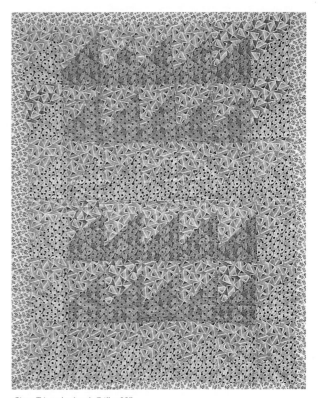

Double Wedding Ring (top). 72" x 80".
Maker unknown. Collection of Roberta Horton, Berkeley, California.
Machine pieced and hand quilted.

Giant Triangles (top). 74" x 82".
Maker unknown.
Collection of the author. Machine pieced.

Using Prints

The busy novelty, geometric, and floral prints are often what attract people to or repel people from this time period. Individually, some are wonderful and some are horrid (depending on your taste, of course). Many of these different fabrics can be used together, but it often helps to mix in some solids to give the eye a place to rest.

I own a top that is pieced with large triangles of print fabric. While I love some of the individual prints, the over-all effect is muddled because the quilt is made up of one print after another. There is no place for the eye to rest as it moves from triangle to triangle. Maybe this is the reason the top was never quilted.

Linear Patterns

In addition to the typical prints, linear designs such as plaids, stripes, and checks were also used. They added variety and helped to compliment the busy prints.

I am particularly enamored with the stripes and diagonal plaids that were used. I have a good-size collection of feed sack and vintage fabric examples that are stripes and diagonal plaids because I have made an effort to collect them. (I have to force myself to buy the printed feed sacks.) Make yourself look for stripes and diagonal plaids and add them to the stack of feed sack, vintage, or reproduction prints you are purchasing to give more variety in your quilts.

Sometimes contemporary stripes can be used if the colors are right. However, many that are available today are curved or abstract stripes (see page 20). The colors are perfect, but something about the design reads contemporary rather than vintage. As far as I'm concerned, you can add them—just be aware that you are not making an exact reproduction, but rather your own interpretation.

Log Cabin (top). 76" x 92".
Maker unknown.
Collection of Susan Dague,
Piedmont, California.
Foundation pieced onto
old work clothes.

Detail of Log Cabin

component parts of a quilt

Like the chapters of a book, there are different structural parts of a quilt that go together to create the whole.

Quilt block patterns were available in syndicated newspaper columns and magazines. An enormous number of new designs were being published. Newer mid-twentieth-century fabrics were also used in classic blocks like Log Cabin (among others).

Sashing was not included in many quilts from the mid-twentieth century. Blocks were often butted one next to the other or set on-point. If the blocks were sashed, the rule was "keep it simple." (My grandmother's Dresden Plate quilt which is shown in full on page 36 is a good example.)

"Keep it simple" was also a good motto for quilt borders. Many quilts were made without borders and just ended with the binding. If borders were added, they were often very uncomplicated—a plain fabric border was adequate. (Look again at my grandmother's quilt on page 36.)

A fancier border treatment could be achieved by attaching a border of plain fabric to the quilt and then adding a border of joined squares or joined triangles. A second plain border was sometimes added. (Examples can be found on pages 30 and 34.)

Occasionally borders were just a little fancier with a simple repeated motif. (See photographs on pages 14 and 39.)

design approach

The vintage quilts in this book are scrap quilts that include many, many fabrics. Women chose fabrics from their scrap bags, traded with friends, and even bought factory scraps by the pound. When they ran out of one fabric, they substituted another similar-but-different fabric. Please remember that it is okay to mend, patch, and even cut off-grain if necessary.

Today, fabric is more plentiful and readily available. We make quilts for pleasure, not usually out of necessity. When we run out of a particular fabric, we are apt to go buy more yardage even though we probably have a huge "stash" of fabric at home already.

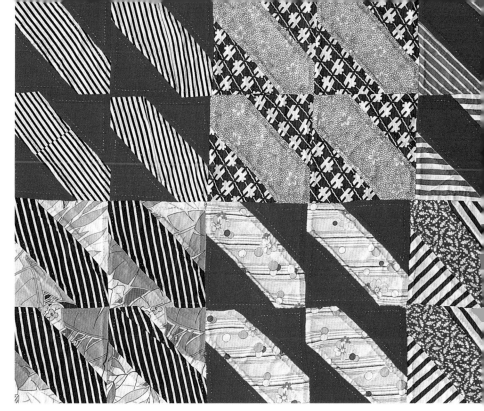

Detail of *Indian Hatchet*. Maker unknown. Collection of Susan Dague, Piedmont, California (quilt shown on page 17). Pieces cut "any which way."

Detail of *Grandmother's Gift*. Gay Nichols (quilt shown on page 53), Albany, California. Four of these squares have been pieced.

Mended feed sack

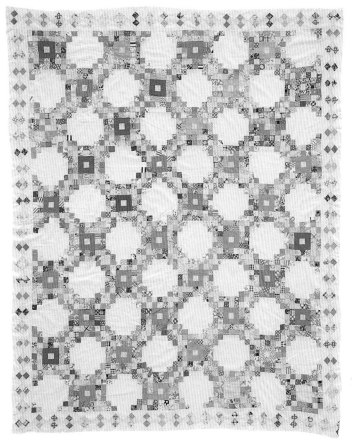

finding rules

You will find that each quilt in the book is based on a set of rules that its creator made up. Some of the rules are harder to figure out than others, but each one helps the quilt make sense visually. It is fun trying to discover what the rules are.

For example, let's look at *Double Irish Chain*. Many, many print fabrics were used. However, a rule is that the center connecting chain is made of pale, solid yellow squares. Even though it is a fairly weak color, the yellow adds a soft glow to the quilt.

What really catches our attention are the darker, solid squares surrounding the yellow square in the center of each large patched square (another rule). The solids give our eyes a resting spot amid the chaos of busy prints. The solid-color rule is broken in several blocks. (The maker probably ran out of solid fabric.) These squares are much harder to see, but add interest to the quilt and make it slightly less rigid. A rule needs to be followed most of the time for the quilt to make sense, but occasionally breaking a rule is alright.

If we look at *Diamond Scrap Quilt* we see that the only rule is that any piece of fabric can be placed next to any other piece of fabric as long as it isn't the same fabric or the same color.

Double Irish Chain (top). 72" x 80". Maker unknown. Hand pieced. Collection of Susan Dague, Piedmont, California.

Diamond Scrap Quilt. 65" x 85". Maker unknown. Hand pieced by maker and hand quilted by Susan Dague in 1980. Collection of Susan Dague, Piedmont, California.

In *Honeycomb Tumblers* the quilter made a rule and then ran out of fabric. Red gingham tumblers made a bold color statement on the left side of the quilt, but when there was no more gingham to cut, a blue print was substituted on the right side. The blue print doesn't stand out in the same way. Notice, however, the conscious effort the quilter made to tie the two disparate parts of the quilt together rather than just make one half red and the other half blue. Our anonymous quilter came up with a much more thrilling solution to "running out."

Brave World offers another solution to running out. The rule is to make as many blocks as you can from a fabric combination. When you run out, move on to something else and do the same. The quilt is made of five strips of blocks. Like-blocks are grouped together.

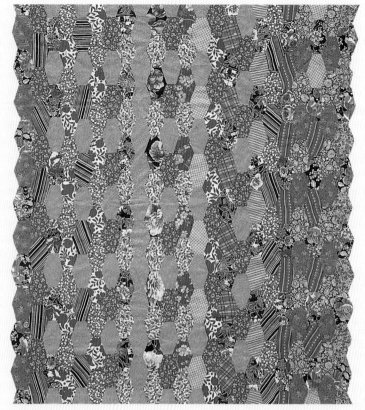

Honeycomb Tumblers (top). 67" x 79". Maker unknown. Machine pieced by maker. Collection of Susan Dague, Piedmont, California.

Brave World. 66" x 77". Maker unknown. Hand and machine pieced, hand quilted. Collection of Carolie A. Hensley, Walnut Creek, California.

Reproduction Eight-Pointed Star Quilt.
45" x 45". 2000. Mary Mashuta.
Machine pieced and quilted.

Let's look at a quilt made with reproduction fabrics that I began some time ago. I intended for it to look like a replica of an old quilt from the '30s. The prints were just another kind of fabric that could be used with stripes. I was unhappy with the results and put it aside.

Then later I decided to make a few changes and see if I could finish it for this book. This quilt was made before I really became "aware."

Let's examine the quilt to see what works and what doesn't.

What works:

    1. Fabric usage—works; all reproductions or acceptable time-period fabrics were used.

    2. Sashing and posts—good.

    3. Borders—none, works.

    4. Color—works, even included bubblegum pink.

Acceptable elements:

    1. Pattern—not one of the most popular, but okay.

    2. Piecing—done by machine, even though many old quilts were hand pieced.

Dead Give-Aways (that it wasn't an exact replica):

    1. Size and shape—wallhanging not bed size, not even small bed size (quilts from the '30s were always functional).

    2. Background fabrics in negative space are too symmetrical and planned.

    3. Quilting—machine quilted rather than traditional hand quilting. Each pattern piece in the blocks would have been outlined ¼" all the way around. Only white thread would have been used.

    4. Design approach—too planned, not a scrap quilt.

The last area is the biggest give-away. I have been clever and used more than one colorway of several prints. My stars are composed from sets of matching fabrics. The blocks have been laid out in an obvious manner—the four corner blocks match, the middle-position side blocks all match, and the odd-color block has been placed in the middle of the quilt.

The conclusion reached is that I tried to make a replica of an old quilt using reproduction fabrics, but I designed and made it like someone living at the end of the twentieth century, not like someone living in 1935.

paying attention

Let's see what we can learn from some vintage quilts and the new quilts they inspired.

In Susan Dague's vintage quilt *Indian Hatchet*, the quilt rule is simple—you make four matching two-fabric blocks to form the basic design unit. If you start running out of fabric, you forget about cutting on grain; you patch, you substitute something similar, you do anything necessary to get your four matching blocks.

I was working with Mabel's scrap bag (page 6) and my assorted vintage bits and pieces. Once I let go of having the blocks all perfectly alike, the process was fun. Cutting stripes off grain, and haphazardly patching them, adds visual excitement to the quilt. Also notice how sometimes the negative space doesn't stay in the background.

Indian Hatchet. 72" x 83". Maker unknown. Hand pieced by maker and hand quilted by Mrs. William Brenneman. Collection of Susan Dague, Piedmont.

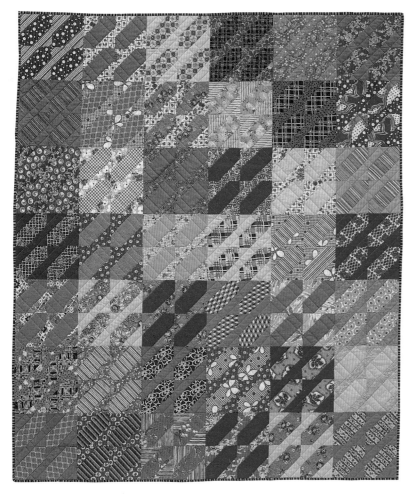

Indian Hatchet. 53¹/₂" x 63".
2000. Mary Mashuta.
Machine pieced by Mary and
machine quilted by Barbara Wilson.

Propeller. 74" x 104".
Maker unknown. Hand quilted.
Collection of Becky Keck,
Martinez, California.

This vintage *Propeller* quilt is a good example of using solids as well as prints. I found five blocks with incorrect piecing. Can you find all of them? I think these mistakes make the quilt more interesting.

This was another perfect project for Mabel's scrap bag and my assorted bits and pieces of vintage fabrics. The block requires only two pattern pieces—a square and a triangle. It is easy to cut using traditional templates. (It's even faster with rotary cutting and fabric stacking.) Sewing takes a little more concentration.

I decided it was time to involve Sonya Barrington who had given me her grandmother Mabel's scraps. I had purposely saved the green and lavender prints because there were a lot of them. Sonya hand dyes and marbles fabric, so she brought her hand-dyed samples, and we picked a lavender for the background triangles and squares. She also dyed a green value gradation for me to use in the crosses.

The quilt didn't seem to work until Rebecca Rohrkaste, my assistant, suggested I see what the blocks looked like on point! That was all it took.

Mabel, Sonya, and Mary. 55¹/₂" x 63".
1999. Mary Mashuta.
Machine pieced and quilted.

I purchased a vintage Old Maid's Puzzle block somewhere along the way. Two of the four fabrics used in the block were dots; a multicolor dot was used for the negative space and a two-color dot was used for the two large triangles.

For fun, I decided to see what I could do with my feed sack and vintage dot collection. I found dot fabrics that would work in the background, sashing, and posts. The hardest thing for me was not co-ordinating the dots used in the triangles of each block. It actually helped that I didn't have unlimited fabric to work with. I had to make-do and use most of what I had. The quilt was quilted with a Baptist Fan design. I am pleased with the results, even though I have never seen a real mid-century quilt made exclusively with dots.

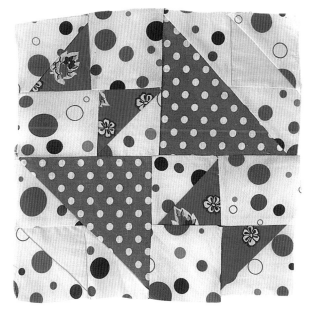

Old Maid's Puzzle block. Collection of the author.

Lots of Dots. 38" x 50".
2000. Mary Mashuta.
Machine pieced and quilted.

Not So Many Dots. 26" x 26".
2000. Mary Mashuta.
Machine pieced and quilted.

I then decided to see what could be done with the limited supply of reproduction dots in my collection. Once again I had to make-do with what I had when I pieced the blocks. At last I was able to find the perfect place for an Art Deco dot fabric I had been saving. It made great sashing. A student gave me a scrap of another colorway of the print that was just large enough to use for the posts. (You would never see this done in an older quilt.) I also decided a tangerine solid made a more colorful background than muslin would have.

Then I asked Rebecca Rohrkaste to stitch her version of the quilt with fabrics from my reproduction prints. She went to the Rhode Island School of Design and has a beautiful color sense. Notice that she used a diagonal plaid in the negative space of the blocks. (You could only get away with this with a light-value plaid.) The sashing is color appropriate, but the wavy lines of the stripes give them away as contemporary stripes. Rebecca followed the tradition of making do with what was available.

Rebecca's Puzzle. 26" x 26".
2000. Rebecca Rohrkaste, Berkeley, California.
Machine pieced by maker and machine quilted by Mary Mashuta.
Collection of the author.

Detail of *Bow Ties and Squares*

Bow Ties and Squares. 70" x 83".
Maker unknown. Hand pieced top.
Collection of Susan Dague, Piedmont, California.

The rules are simple in Susan Dague's vintage *Bow Ties and Squares* top even though it is a scrap quilt and many fabrics were used—the Bow Tie blocks (2³/₄") are on-point and are alternated with plain squares. The layout is more complicated, however. Visually the Bow Ties are colored in vertical rows. Each row has a fairly consistent Bow Tie color, but there is quite a variety of colors and, especially, fabrics in the background pieces in the blocks. The squares are also produced in sets, but the colors run in diagonal rows—not vertical or horizontal!

Bow Ties for George and Roger. Machine pieced fragment. Mary Mashuta.

I am working on my version of *Bow Ties and Squares.* Friends cut squares and bow ties to make 3¹/₂" blocks, which I am stitching and arranging on my design wall.

conclusion

Quilts can be carefully planned with a limited amount of coordinated fabrics (fabric lines are specifically designed to go together) or quilts can be designed more intuitively and spontaneously. Studying the older quilts pictured in this book, as I did, can help you to be more willing to accept substitutes when you run out of fabric. In the end, when everything doesn't match exactly, you will find your quilts becoming more exciting and interesting.

Quilts Using Squares

It's not necessary to make complicated quilts to be able to enjoy feed sacks, vintage fabrics, and reproduction prints. Sometimes "less is more." Blocks based on simple combinations of squares are a good place to start. They can be rotary cut without drafting the block first, and the pieces are easy to move around while you are composing the quilt. A simple first project can build confidence in using these busy fabrics. The quilt becomes a trial run, which gives you experience and makes more complex projects less threatening later on.

The busy nature of the print fabrics makes it easy to lose block definition when the quilt is viewed as a whole. Some blurring is fine, but there has to be somewhere that the viewer can look and say, "Yes, that makes sense, I can tell what block and set is being used." Concentrating on making sense in early, simple projects makes it possible to be more artful in the future. We want to help the quilt viewer to always be able to figure out what is going on.

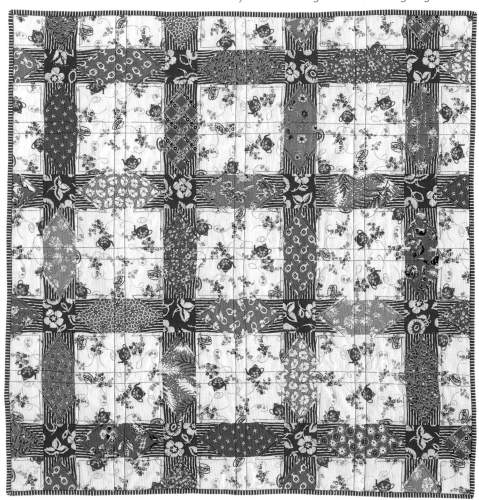

Susan Dague originally planned to use eight-inch squares of her pink and her blue feed sack and vintage fabrics with blue and red sashing built around Eight-Pointed Stars. However, when she put them together there was too much happening, so she decided to separate these two elements (the eight-inch squares and the blue and red sashing) into two quilts.

For the first quilt, Susan found a white background floral print to use with the sashing. The stars could stand out as repeating stars, and the many blue prints in the sashing that joined the stars could also be enjoyed. There aren't as many things to confuse the eyes. Notice the binding, too. Susan has repeated the stripe she used in the star points.

Eight-Pointed Star Lattice. 41 1/2" x 41 1/2".
2000. Susan Dague, Piedmont, California.
Machine pieced and machine quilted.

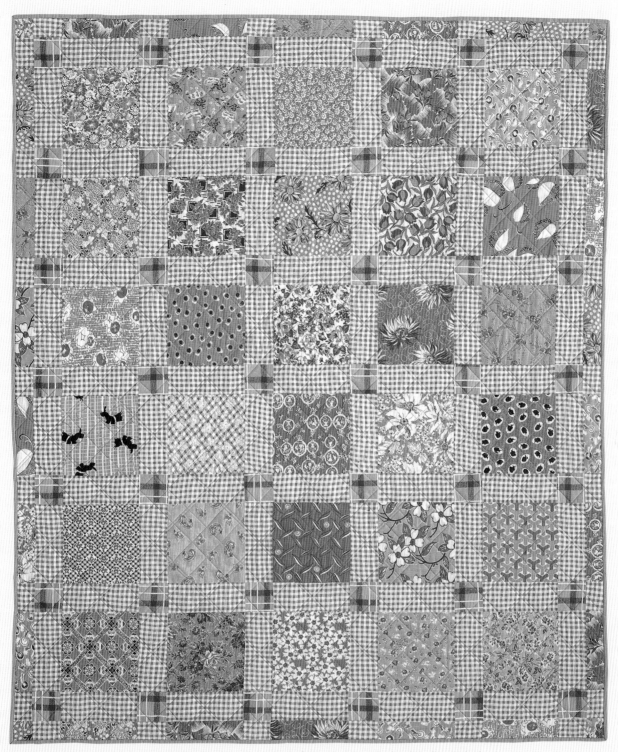

Blue Check Sashed Squares. 61" x 72". 1999. Susan Dague, Piedmont, California. Machine pieced and machine quilted.

The pink print squares showed off better with a non-competing, blue checked sashing. She used a large plaid for the posts. Rather than "fussy-cutting" the posts (placing the same part of the pattern in each square), she just let the cuts fall where they would as she rotary cut the squares from strips. This added a more playful note to the sashing and is in keeping with a tradition of little or no waste. Notice how a green binding picks up the color green in the plaid posts.

In the end, one very busy quilt evolved into two less complicated ones. In one quilt the sashing is more important than the squares. In the other, the squares are more important than the sashing.

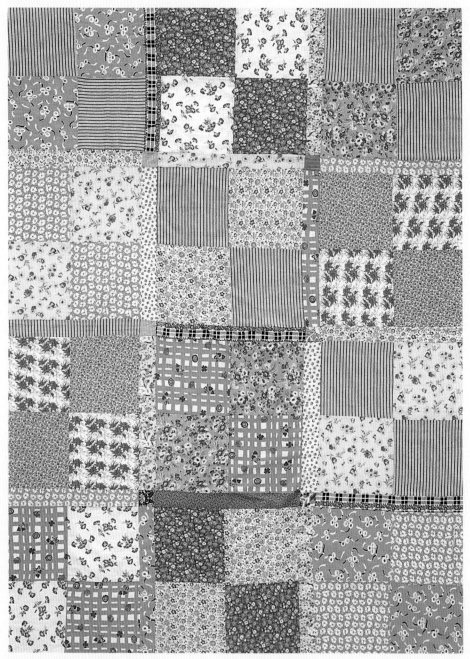

Anita's Giant Four-Patch (top). 66" x 89".
Anita Fasano (1892-1976). San Francisco, California.
Hand pieced. Collection of Susan Dague, Piedmont, California.

A small label attached to *Anita's Giant Four-Patch* tells us that Anita Fasano was born in Germany, and that she was 84 years old when she died in San Francisco in 1976. It is a collection of twenty-inch blocks joined by two-inch sashing. Anita used two prints for each block. She didn't mind using the same fabrics in more than one block or using the same fabrics again in the sashing if necessary. The top was definitely a "make-do," "use-it-up" kind of project. It is informal and welcoming.

This would be a great quilt to make for people who collect feed sack squares. All you have to do to create the individual Four-Patch blocks is group four same-color squares together. Many quilters buy individual feed sack squares but never really get to have the fun of using them. It is easy to get attached to the preciousness of the fabric.

Hint: Base the block size on the smallest square in your collection, then trim the remainder to this size. I usually trim the squares to 5½" x 5½", so I end up with 5" squares when they are stitched into a block.

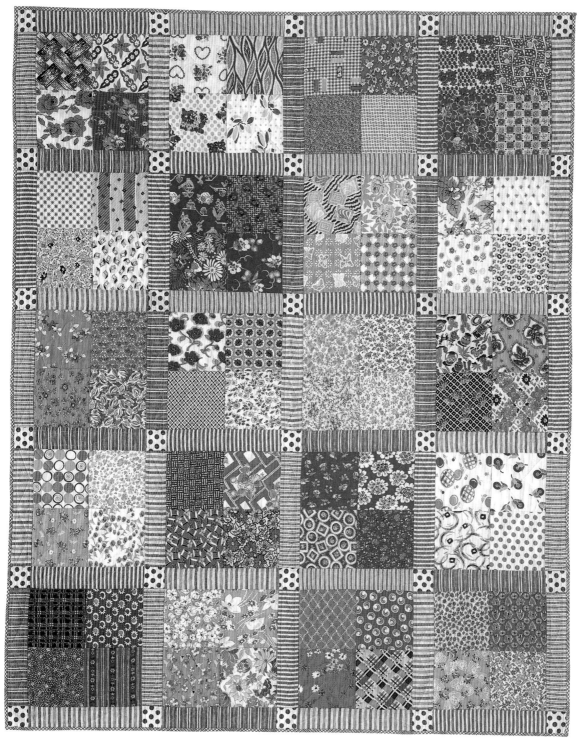

Nebraska Giant Four-Patch. 54" x 67". 2000. Mary Mashuta. Machine pieced and quilted.

Nebraska Giant Four-Patch uses some of the first feed sack squares I purchased in the early 1990s. I bought them in color coordinated packages of six. (They were purchased as hostess gifts for a trip abroad, but I couldn't give them up once I got them home.)

Since I collect feed sack and vintage stripes, I was able to find four red-and-white ones for my sashing. This gave me enough fabric, but also made the sashing more interesting than if I had used only one fabric. The stripes were a good pattern change from the prints in my squares. A blue-and-white polka dot print gave a color change and pattern contrast for the sashing posts, and a blue-white-and-red diagonal plaid was used for the binding.

Sometimes we don't have the luxury of big pieces of fabric. Kathy Sward purchased antique Four-Patch blocks while on a trip back home to Kansas. To create *There's No Place Like Home, There's No Place Like Home* she sewed the pieced squares together in a diagonal pattern and bordered them with a floral feed sack and a vintage stripe. Believe it or not, she then added a large-scale print she purchased in Japantown in San Francisco! It's not a feed sack or vintage fabric, but it certainly looks great and it fooled me. The red check binding brings out the red in the quilt.

The Nine-Patch block requires nine squares: five of one color, four of a second. You don't get much plainer than that, and yet there have been an endless number of beautiful and different nine-patch quilts created.

Susan Dague shared one of these quilts with me, and I immediately noticed a variation in the blocks that would be perfect for vintage fabric buyers. The maker of Susan's quilt used four squares of the first color, four squares of the second color, and added a ninth "other color" square in the middle. She set the blocks with alternating red squares.

There's No Place Like Home, There's No Place Like Home. 36" x 36¹/₂".
1992. Kathy Sward, Muir Beach, California.
Machine pieced and hand quilted.

Red Nine-Patch. Maker unknown.
80" x 84". Collection of Susan Dague,
Piedmont, California. Hand pieced top.

I made a copy of Susan's quilt top using fabrics from the scrap bag of Sonya Barrington's grandmother. I used one of the large pieces of green for my alternate squares. It was fun realizing that each block didn't have to be beautiful for the quilt to work. This concept is also a revelation for my students when I have them make a group copy of my quilt, *Mabel's Nine-Patch*.

The "alternate square" concept allows you to make your multi-fabric Nine-Patch blocks match any room. I made a second quilt with reproduction fabrics and used peach for the alternate squares.

Peach Nine-Patch. 26" x 26".
1999. Mary Mashuta.
Machine pieced and machine quilted.

Mabel's Nine-Patch. 52½" x 60½".
2000. Mary Mashuta.
Machine pieced top.

Rita Kilstrom was determined to make a non-pastel nine-patch quilt using reproduction fabrics. She limited herself to red, black, and white prints and used a contemporary, yellow-dot print for her alternate squares. She loves to do redwork and embroidered the squares with a collection of transferred designs. Notice her unmatched print borders and four-patch corners.

Here is yet another nine-patch variation. Alice Lowenthal inherited two twin quilttops from her mother, Mabel Lundin. (One is shown on page 29.) Squares are made up of nine unmatched fabrics. However, the center squares are always green to match the alternate plain squares. It simply doesn't make any difference what eight squares you join together around the outside of the block. It just works.

Happy Baby Quilt. 33" x 41". 1999.
Rita Young Kilstrom, Arnold, California.
Machine pieced, hand and machine quilted,
hand embroidered redwork. Collection of
Kira Catherine Kilstrom Hoover.

Seventies Nine-Patch. 25" x 25".
2000. Machine pieced and quilted.
Mary Mashuta.

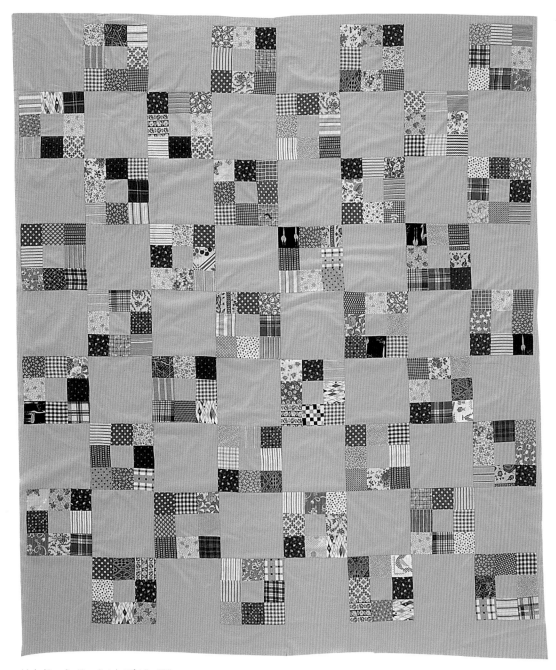

Mabel Lundin Nine-Patch. 70^1/$_2$" x 83".
Maker unknown. Probably Illinois.
Machine pieced and hand appliquéd top.
Collection of the author.

This quilt is a perfect project for quilt guilds to copy as they make community quilts to be given away. A wide assortment of fabric is donated to the guilds for their service projects. It doesn't necessarily go together. Here is a simple way to make it work. Squares can be pre-cut as the fabric comes in. All that is needed is the solid fabric. Squares can be randomly joined or color co-ordinated, whichever the makers prefer. As members assemble the quilts they have the opportunity to do good things for others. As a bonus, they get to play with color.

To test the "anything goes" theory, I made my own small quilt using 1970s calicos and pin dots (page 28). I call it *Seventies Nine-Patch*.

Green Nine-Patch and Snowball. 54" x 54".
2000. Mary Mashuta.
Machine pieced and quilted, embellished with buttons.

Nine-Patch blocks can also be alternated with Snowball blocks which are formed when four triangles are added to the corners of alternate plain squares. To emphasize the corner triangles I cut them from stripes. One stripe was in a set of orange, green, brown, and white prints I purchased as a coordinated package. The package set the color scheme for the quilt. I found the second stripe and more printed fabrics in my collection. I used up three different green solids from my collection for the alternate squares and plain borders. Then I shopped in Susan Dague's stash.

Leftover prints were cut into triangles and joined to form a simple border, which is consistent with the time period. Joined squares were also used.

So far I had adhered to the rules in constructing my quilt because I had used traditional fabric, block pattern, and border design. I deviated by making a square quilt and machine quilting it as I've done in other samples. Then I opted to embellish the completed quilt with orange, vintage buttons. They were sewn into a cable pattern that had been stitched into a plain green border. Safety note: Don't add buttons to quilts that will be used by babies or small children.

Nine-Patch and Diagonal Cross. 31" x 31".
1995. Mary Mashuta.
Machine pieced top.

Plaid Border for Adrian's Nine-Patches top. 41" x 41".
2000. Mary Mashuta.

Many years ago I fell in love with a 1880 nine-patch quilt that used printed Diagonal Cross blocks as the alternate block. For my quilt, I combined a pastel stripe feed sack with hand painted fabric by Adrian Young to make the Diagonal Cross blocks. Feed sack squares were cut into quarters and combined with a commercial hand-painted-look aqua fabric to create the Nine-Patch blocks. The results are beautiful but too pale.

Five years later I returned to the top and the many extra blocks I had pieced. It finally dawned on me that I could salvage the top. It just needed a border to add a little life. A diagonal-plaid feed sack, added to my collection in the meantime, was the solution. Notice that the corner blocks are a different colorway of the same plaid. They were cut from an extra strip of fabric patched to the feed sack to make it the right size.

The other solution I came up with for the pale-but-beautiful blocks was to add purple sashing. Now you can see two solutions for the set of blocks.

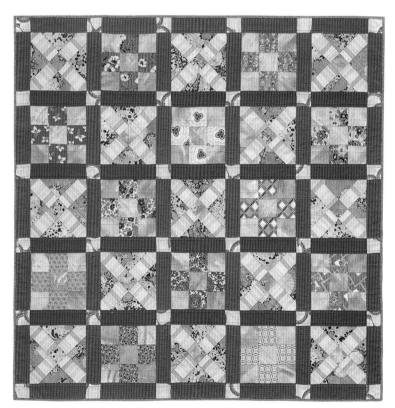

Purple Sashing for Adrian's Nine-Patches. 49 1/2" x 49 1/2".
2000. Mary Mashuta.
Machine pieced and quilted.

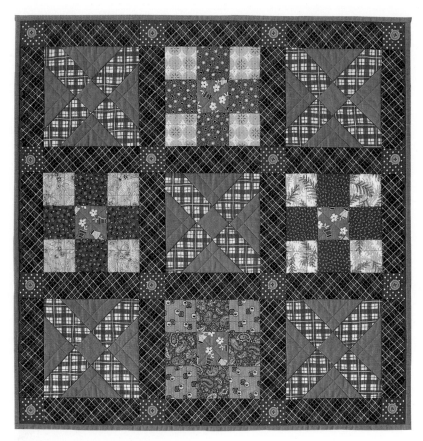

Plaid Diagonal Cross and Nine-Patch. 31" x 31".
2000. Mary Mashuta. Machine pieced and quilted;
embellished with buttons and rickrack.

It is also possible to place a plaid in the Diagonal Cross blocks instead of a stripe. I used a contemporary red-and-white plaid with reproduction-color green triangles for the blocks. The Nine-Patch blocks were made from reproduction 1930s prints and real 1970s calicos from my collection.

Then I added a dark green plaid sashing. The plaid was a straight vertical/horizontal plaid, so I cut it on the bias to simulate traditional diagonally-drawn plaids. (Don't worry about the bias edges. The blocks have mostly straight-cut edges and I stay-stitched the edge of the quilt.)

Just for fun I embellished the polka-dot posts with vintage green buttons and added red rick rack to the edge before I bound the quilt. Safety note: Don't add buttons to quilts which will be used by infants or small children.

You could say Posy Patch is a variation of the Diagonal Cross block. However, it is a Sixteen-Patch block rather than a Four-Patch block. Eight print squares are added along the edge, two to a side. Adjacent blocks just happen to form four-patches when they are stitched together.

Plaid Posy Patch. 32" x 32".
2000. Mary Mashuta.
Machine pieced and quilted.

Stripe Posy Patch. 60" x 60".
2000. Mary Mashuta. Machine pieced and quilted.
Project instructions begin on page 108.

Since I have so many stripes in my feed sack and vintage fabric collection, I had found a block that would give me the opportunity to feature nine different stripes in the nine-block quilt I decided to make. Again, my feed sack squares came in handy. I selected eight same-color squares for each block. The background triangles were cut from a light blue feed sack. The blocks measure 20" square so the quilt grew quickly.

I made a simpler, smaller version with reproduction fabrics—red-and-gold solids, a diagonal plaid, and eight prints. There were four exactly-alike sixteen-inch blocks in the quilt. Of course, if you have a big print collection you could use all different print squares as I did in the feed sack version.

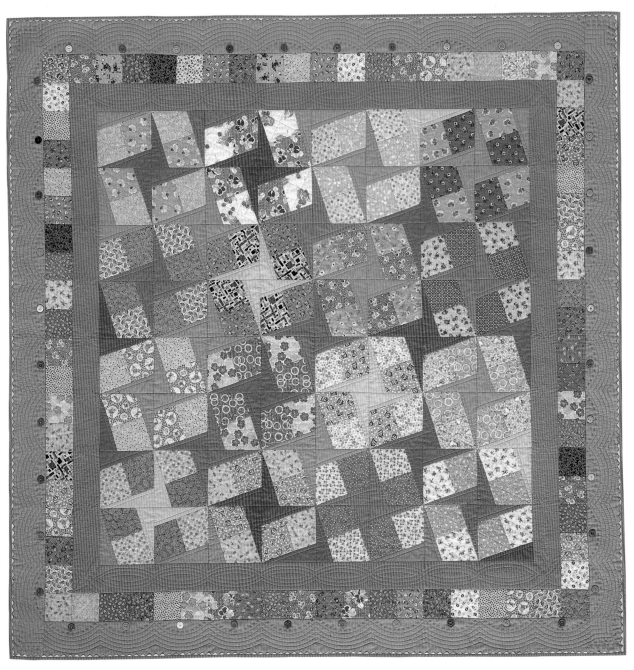

Fiesta Stars. 66¹/₂" x 66¹/₂".
1999. Mary Mashuta. Machine pieced and quilted;
embellished with vintage buttons, variegated rick rack,
and variegated sashiko thread. Project instructions begin on page 89.

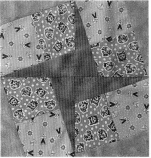

Star and Askew Nine-Patch block.
Star cut from "wispy" solids.

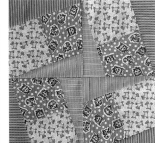

Star and Askew Nine-Patch block.
Star cut from stripes.

While there are countless traditional blocks that work well with the fabric I am exploring and discussing here, you might also enjoy trying a more contemporary block and approach. The beauty of the Star and Askew Nine-Patch block is that it only takes two templates—one for the star and one for the background askew nine-patch.

Visually the stars need to stand out and the nine-patches stay in the background. Using busy prints for both parts of the block won't work. The trick is to make the star a non-print. In the examples shown I have used solids, textures, stripes, and checks. Plaids would also work.

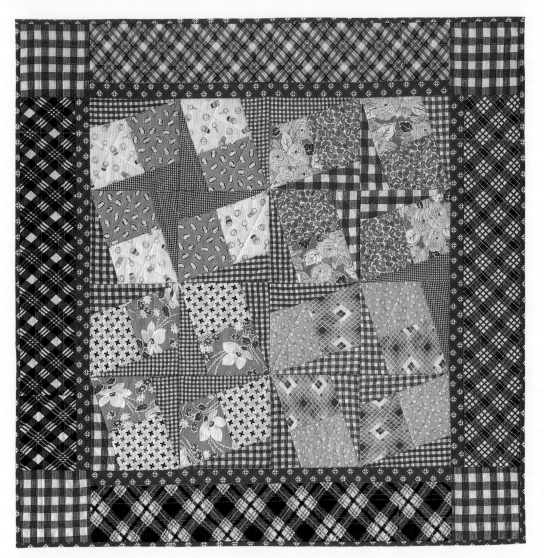

Red Check Stars. 33" x 33".
2000. Mary Mashuta.
Machine pieced and quilted.

The nine-patches which form behind the stars work best when they are cut from medium and light values—one each per block. Place the medium value in the center and the light value at the corners.

The quilt can be simple and end with just binding. However, it is fun to add a border or two. *Fiesta Stars* is a serious piece. I added two plain borders and one joined-square border. However, I chose to abandon tradition and made the plain borders different colors. Then I added lots of quilting and embellishment.

Red Check Stars gave me an opportunity to use the checked fabrics I had been collecting. A small print border was added to separate the stars from the diagonal plaid borders. It was fun to use four similar-but-different plaids. I had just enough of the print fabric left to cut binding. Also notice the four corner blocks. Again, my border treatment is probably a break with tradition .

conclusion

Using simple blocks with few pattern pieces have advantages for the busy fabrics we are using. They allow the fabrics to be the star of the block. The pattern pieces are fast and easy to rotary cut so you can fast forward to the designing. I don't know about you, but for me, this is the fun part.

Quilts Using Curves

You can learn a lot about color and design by limiting yourself to one block pattern and then studying a variety of examples. Before long you begin to see other quilts that are similar, but different.

My maternal grandmother, George McLeod Peterson, pieced and appliquéd Dresden Plate tops for my sister and me. One survives, but the other one was lost along the way. I can remember my mother using the tops to cover the recliner and chaise lounge on our screened 1950s porch. MaMa pinked the sashing/border seams since she intended the tops to be used unquilted. She pieced the tops on the Singer Featherweight portable I later inherited from her. It is comforting to caress the remaining top and know it was made by her.

MaMa's Dresden Plate is a classic, typical example of the pattern. The plates are sewn to a muslin background, and the blocks are joined with a plain sashing that has posts. Black embroidery thread is used to stitch the outer plate edges in place.

In this block, the plates are the positive space and the background muslin is the negative space. The plate wedges are cut from scrap fabrics and should contrast the background. In MaMa's top, some of the fabrics have sun-faded, but others were always white. Even though she had studied art, MaMa probably didn't think about the white wedges "bleeding," or blending into the background.

Within the Dresden Plate classification many possibilities for variation exist. An example in my collection has rounded rather than pointed wedges. It is less typical because it has pink

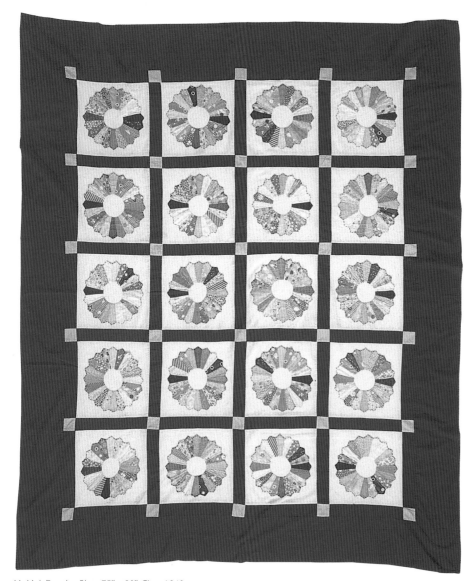

MaMa's Dresden Plate. 75" x 90". Circa 1940.
George McLeod Peterson, Brooksville, Mississippi.
Machine pieced and hand appliquéd top.
Collection of Mary Mashuta and Roberta Horton.

centers, and the plates have been stitched to blue squares. Black herringbone embroidery stitches were used to appliqué both edges of the plates. In the tradition of making-do, the background blocks were cut from a number of different blues. The Art Deco geometric print sashing demands our attention. (Note that there are no posts.)

Going further afield, Sonya Callahan owns a Dresden Plate variation that is quite unique. The block is called Friendship Garden. The eight wedges are pointed and hand stitched to a muslin "petal" background. When four blocks meet, a four-petal flower appears in the negative space. Each has a blue octagon appliquéd center. Sonya rescued the uncompleted squares at a flea market and came up with this solution. The possibility of creating different color, negative-space flowers intrigues me as a contemporary quilter.

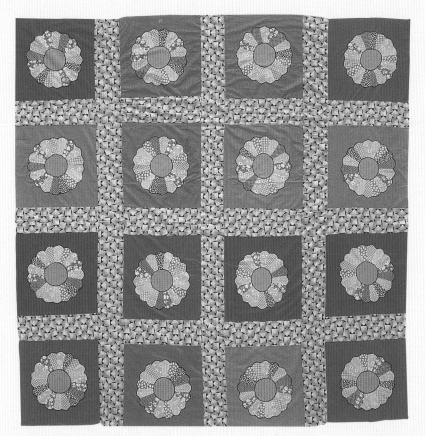

Pink Center Dresden Plate. 84" x 84".
Circa 1930. Maker unknown.
Machine pieced and hand appliquéd top.
Collection of the author.

Detail of *Friendship Garden*

Friendship Garden. 58" x 68$\frac{1}{2}$".
Circa 1930; completed 1983.
Rescued blocks; completion and design
by Sonya Callahan while living in Indonesia;
hand quilted by Latsio Saechao and her sister.

It is also possible to fragment the Dresden Plate block into quarters and create a Fan block. Angie Woolman once owned a quilt that could be called Split Dresden Plate or Sashed Fan, depending on your point of reference. The sashing divides, rather than surrounds, the plates. Blocks are made up of four fans or quarter-circles. Appliquéd floral motifs are placed in the centers of the newly created blocks. Names have been embroidered in all but one of the squares so this must have been some type of presentation quilt.

My sister owns a top with small fans and large backgrounds. I like it because of this atypical imbalance between the positive space (fans) and the negative space (peach background squares). If I had to quilt it, however, there would be lots of background space to fill with stitching.

Fan blocks can be grouped in many ways. I particularly love a yellow-and-green fan quilt in the La Conner Quilt Museum/Jane Jackson Collection. There are a number of design decisions made by the maker that create a lively quilt. The wedges alternate in a light/dark pattern. This adds contrast and creates a staccato pattern. The opposing arrangement of the fans is less expected and, again, makes the quilt more exciting.

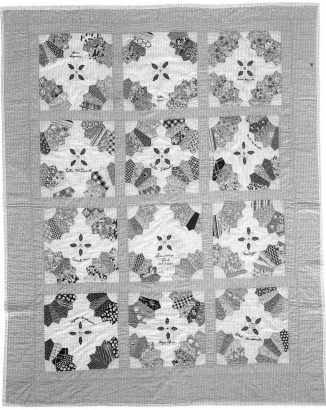

Sashed Fans. 56" x 66".
Circa 1930. Maker unknown.
Owner unknown.

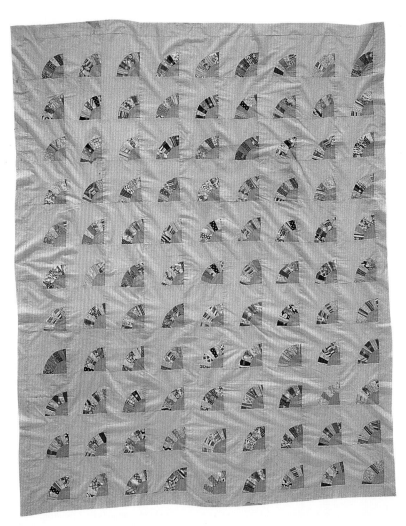

Fans. 74" x 94". Circa 1930.
Maker unknown.
Unquilted top. Collection
of Roberta Horton,
Berkeley, California.

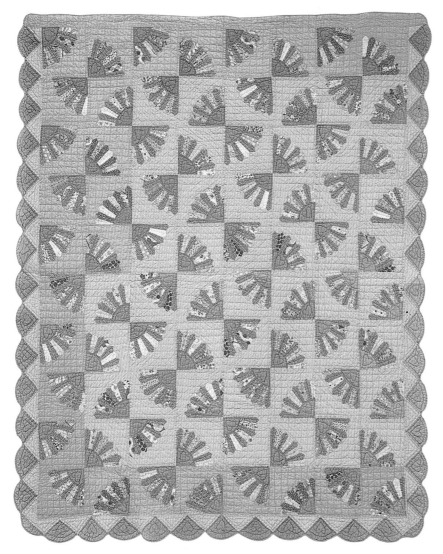

Fans with Green Centers. 66"x 82".
Circa 1930. Hand pieced, appliquéd, and quilted.
From the Jane Jackson Collection,
La Conner Quilt Museum, La Conner, Washington.

Serpentine Fans. 19" x 31".
Late 1980s. Mary Mashuta. Machine pieced,
hand appliquéd unfinished quilt top.

Notice that the green, quarter-circle fan centers repeat at the quilt edge to make a charming three-sided border. The maker ran out of her yellow background fabric and had to make do.

In the late 1980s, I stitched fans to muslin hand-painted by Stacy Michell for *Serpentine Fans*. This muslin is so much prettier and livelier than plain muslin.

I combined 1930s reproduction fabrics purchased in Japan with real vintage fabrics from Mabel's scrap bag (page 6). I favored a serpentine arrangement of the blocks. My sister has bugged me to finish this top for years and years, but it is taking a long time for me to figure out what to do with the background when I quilt it.

I fell in love with Susan Dague's *Red Baskets* quilt (page 40) the moment I saw it on her living room wall. Since I am attracted to circles and fans, I immediately realized that the baskets were made from fan wedges. Within the limitation of the five wedge arc, the maker tried a number of different fabric combinations. Some, but not all, are two-fabric baskets. Many of these baskets combine a print with a solid. Other baskets are made from five different prints and no solids. In other words, the maker made up several design rules to try out. In the final placement, the baskets are all mixed up, but this design quirk makes for a lively quilt.

A red triangle border repeats the red used in the basket handles and bases. The contrast between the red and muslin colors creates a strong zigzag line that further adds to the playful feeling of the quilt.

Red Baskets. 68" x 82".
Machine pieced by maker and hand quilted by Mrs. William Brenneman in 1996.
Collection Susan Dague, Piedmont, California.

Rainbow Baskets. 34¹/₂" x 34¹/₂".
2000. Susan Dague, Piedmont, California.
Machine pieced, hand and machine quilted.
Project instructions begin on page 101.

Susan decided to make her own smaller version of the quilt. I encouraged her to use a pastel color for the background rather than muslin, and she selected a peach feed sack. She decided to try a charm quilt approach (each wedge a different piece of fabric) since she owns so many prints.

Since the quilt is much smaller than the one that inspired it, Susan opted for just filling in the border triangles with the background fabric. A contrasting zigzag border would have been too strong because it would have overpowered the baskets, which Susan wanted to be the most important part of the quilt.

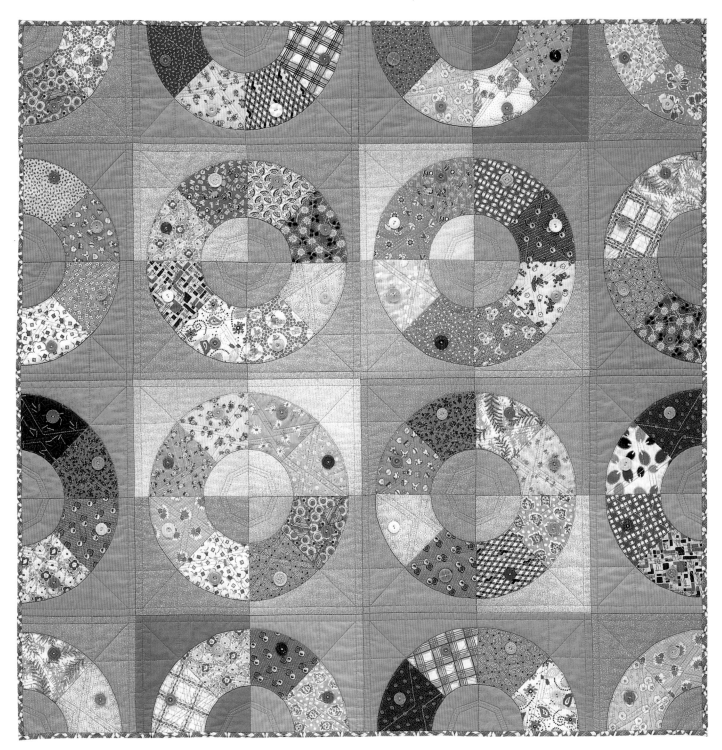

Circle Within Circle. 45^1/$_2$" x 45^1/$_2$".
1999. Mary Mashuta. Machine pieced and appliquéd. Machine quilted with rayon and perle cotton threads. Embellished with vintage buttons.
Project instructions begin on page 87.

Pastel Circle Within Circle. 30" x 30".
2000. Mary Mashuta. Machine pieced and
appliquéd. Machine quilted with rayon and
perle cotton threads. Embellished with
vintage buttons.

I had tried one Dresden Plate quilt, but I wanted a simpler version my students could be more artful with when I taught classes. *Circle Within Circle* filled the bill. I first found the block in a 1970 leaflet my sister and I have. Traditionally the pieced rings were sewn to solid blocks, but it dawned on me that I could divide each background square into four smaller squares. Using a different color for each of the four new squares would make the background (negative space) a lot more interesting.

The pieced background, cut from Pointillist Palette pastels, quickly updated the look of the blocks. When I ran out of fabric, I switched to using pastel solids from my collection. These were placed behind the half rings at the edge of the quilt. Grouping the "extras" in an organized manner, rather than randomly scattering them, makes them less noticeable.

I had fun embellishing the quilt with perle cotton stitching and vintage buttons.

Later I made a simpler version of the quilt in which I used Fossil Fern© prints in the pieced background. In the first version of the quilt I had been able to use a few white-background prints in the ring segments. In the second quilt, the subtle, non-print background colors were paler and offered less contrast to the rings. I soon discovered that segments cut from white-background prints blended into the paler background as the white segments had in my grandmother's quilt top. They had to be replaced with fabrics that offered stronger contrast.

Backing fabric of *Out-of-Sight Circles*

Making one more version of the quilt allowed me to use some '60s/'70s prints and play with background again. I had purchased a round, daisy-print tablecloth in Lithopolis, Ohio for three dollars which would make a great border. I decided to combine it with a crazy-quilt-style piece of fabric that contained all the prints you see in the rings. All I had to do was find fabrics to use for the background.

A hand-dyed-look aqua fabric provided the perfect background for the rings. It picked up colors in the ring fabrics but provided a strong contrast. The rings could have been appliquéd to the whole piece of fabric, but it was much more interesting to fragment it by cutting it into squares as I had on the previous quilts. In this way large swirls of color that would have caught the viewer's eye were broken up.

Notice how a tiny inner border of orange-and-white stripe fabric provides a good pattern contrast between the rings and border print. Without it the prints would have "mushed" together. Diagonal plaid feed sack corners bring the inner background color to the outside of the quilt. They also provide a welcome pattern contrast. Borders don't just make a quilt the right size; they provide an opportunity to improve what is happening in the middle of the quilt.

One day while rummaging around in file drawers, I discovered a "to die for" print to use for the back of the quilt. This was the perfect final touch.

Out-of-Sight Circles. 40" x 40". 2000. Mary Mashuta.
Machine pieced and appliquéd. Machine quilted with rayon
and perle cotton threads. Embellished with vintage buttons.

If you would like to try a more complicated circle, try the Wagon Wheel block. It takes a little more patience to construct the blocks and join them to each other, but it is worth it.

Susan Dague owns a quilt top which is a classic example. It is a true scrap quilt. The more prints you have available for the spokes, the better. Muslin is used for the background and the center circles are appliquéd with a variety of solids. The circles provide a resting spot for the eye, but since they are made from many colors, the eye quickly moves on.

I asked George Taylor to draft the block for me. When I e-mailed him to find out why he hadn't carried out his assignment, he e-mailed back a picture of his quilt top! What a surprise! His version has blue center circles. This is a good example of how you could make your quilt match a particular room while still being made from a wide assortment of prints. The background spokes could have also been cut from a color rather than using muslin.

Detail of *Wagon Wheel* (top).
Maker unknown. Collection of Susan Dague,
Piedmont, California. Hand pieced.

Blue Wagon Wheel. 51^1/$_2$" x 72^1/$_2$".
1999. George Taylor, Anchorage, Alaska.
Machine pieced and quilted.

Check Wagon Wheel. 38" x 36¹/₂".
2000. Mary Mashuta. Machine pieced, appliquéd, and quilted.
Project instructions begin on page 93.

Traditionally Wagon Wheel is made from scraps and muslin, but there are other possible fabric combinations. I made two quilts to prove this. For the first one, I used reproduction fabrics for the spokes and pieced them with a checked background. Since the printed check came in five colorways, I used all five. Individual wheels are limited to a one-color look—a same-color checked background and six different, but color-matched prints. Now the individual blocks stand out more.

YoYo Wagon Wheels. 62" x 66".
2000. Mary Mashuta.
Machine pieced top.

For the second quilt I, at last, had found a block worthy of my feed sack and vintage stripe collection. Traditionally each spoke in the block is a different print, but I had enough stripes to make many one-stripe blocks. To complement my stripes, I purchased 1950s vintage solids from the Kirk Collection. They had many, many solids and I had many, many stripes. Who could ask for more?

While I was in a creative frenzy, I realized that I could use vintage yoyos for the center circles. Circles are circles. There is no rule that says they have to be flat, ordinary circles.

conclusion

There were many wonderful quilts made during the time period we are studying. Concentrating on circle-type blocks makes us more aware of how the component parts of the block in similar-but-different quilts add to the final impact of the finished quilt.

More Inspiration

Here is more inspiration to stimulate you to create your own project. Maybe you will begin with your own collection or be encouraged to purchase some vintage fabrics. Let's have a look.

Sometimes a little detective work is required to track down a great quilt. A friend sent me a photo she had taken at a quilt show. I used a magnifying glass to make out the quilt name and entry number on the quilt label and eventually ended up meeting Gwen Maule who had purchased the quilt as a top. It was made by an elderly lady in Oregon, and the fabrics are probably '40s or '50s. Unfortunately, Gwen doesn't know the name of the maker.

Prairie Queen is a busy, happy celebration of fabric. The quilt has a certain confused quality about it that I love. The sashing separating the rows of horizontal blocks is made up of joined, printed squares rather than long rectangular strips of fabric. I can only guess why the quilt was put together in this way. Did the maker not have a large enough piece of fabric for the sashing, did she have more blocks than she needed, or did the math not quite work out to make the quilt the desired width and length without a little adjusting? Who knows? Maybe the quilter wasn't happy with her solution and consequently never quilted the top. Happily, the problem was solved as far as I'm concerned.

Gwen was inspired to make a calmer wallhanging-size version of her vintage top. She combined reproduction fabrics with a feed sack and several vintage prints and sashed the blocks with a one-print plain sashing in *Prairie Queen #2*. Notice that the sashing posts were cut from different fabrics. This helps to add subtle life to the softer feeling quilt.

Prairie Queen #2. 44" x 44". 1999.
Gwen Maule, Rancho Cordova, California.
Machine pieced and hand quilted in
Baptist Fan pattern.

Prairie Queen. 72 ¹/₂" x 96".
Maker unknown, Springfield, Oregon.
Hand pieced by maker and hand quilted in Baptist Fan pattern by Gwen Maule.
Collection of Gwen Maule, Rancho Cordova, California.

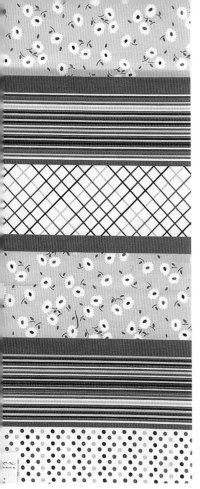

Fabric manufactured by Crantex.

Laura Delaney and her mother, Eloise Reeves, were instrumental in getting Giny Dixon started in quiltmaking. Laurie gave Giny her first "cheater cloth" for a baby quilt, and Eloise gave Giny quilting books and excess fabric when she relocated from the Bay Area to Oregon. When Giny enrolled in one of my Stripes Go Contemporary classes, she brought along a piece of fabric given to her by Eloise. It was probably a '60s border print which Giny says, ". . . reminds me of my mother's kitchen when I was young and my first apartment kitchen." Giny decided to call her quilt '60s Kitchen Colors.

The fabric was a good place for Giny to start her quilt. Eloise's border print featured a stripe, a window pane plaid, a floral, and a dot pattern in repeating rows. Additional 1990s fabrics were added to provide sufficient fabric for the project. The two-template block lends itself to many configurations, but Giny decided to keep it simple and go for a straightforward diagonal set.

Giny enjoyed manipulating her fabric placement to get the end result she was looking for—a balance between calmness and liveliness. She made a few rules for herself. Diagonal plaid and dot rows were always pattern-consistent within their rows so they would add a calming effect. Yellow was the designated color for the quarter circles, but the original yellow print is alternated with a wide variety of other yellow stripes and prints. This adds more life to the quilt than just endlessly repeating one print. Finally, the original stripe is mixed with six other stripes that complement it.

Adding fabrics stretched the available fabric so Giny had enough for a quilt, but the additional fabrics also made the quilt much more interesting. This is a good example of "more is better." We consistently see the addition of more, but similar, fabrics in older quilts. Because fabric is more plentiful today and we can buy more if we run out, we often miss the opportunity of making do, or extending what we have, a principal which makes old quilts interesting.

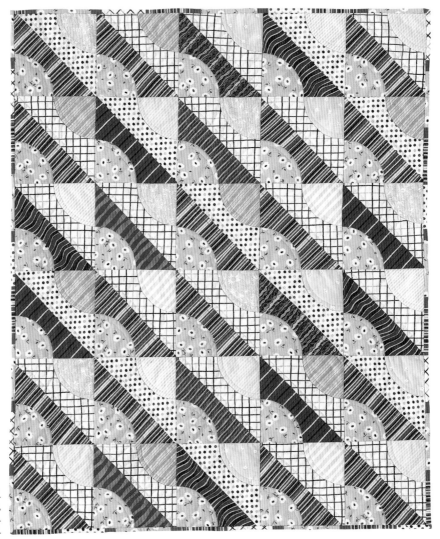

'60s Kitchen Colors. 34" x 41".
1999. Giny Dixon,
Danville, California.
Machine pieced and quilted.

Quilts and quilt tops that are handed down to us in our families put us in touch with our ancestors, even if we never knew them. Gram Latz gave Becky Keck several parts of a top that was pieced by Becky's great grandmother, Daisy George. Family history tells us that Daisy came to this country from Holland as a child. She was a school teacher who spoke seven languages. She was a great story teller and was in demand at school and social gatherings for this and her musical abilities. Never heard of her being much of a seamstress.

At first Becky contemplated trying to sew the two fragments together and quilt the top. This would have been a real challenge! We decided it might be better for her to make her own version and just cherish the pieces she had inherited.

Becky's quilt is laid out in two repeating design bands. One band consists of large squares alternating with four-patches. The other band is made up of strips of squares and triangles. Daisy used a pink fabric for her squares, but Becky decided to use a wide assortment of solids in the blue-to-green range instead. We could say that Becky followed the scrap tradition of making-do and using up her fabric, or we could say she was being artful in the manner of someone who has made contemporary art quilts. The wide assortment of blues and greens makes her quilt lively. Daisy's is more static visually because she limited herself to one repeated color.

The quilt was a great way for Becky to make a project with the reproduction fabrics in her collection. She followed tradition and threw in anything else that seemed to work.

Pieced top fragment. 38" x 84".
"Daisy" Hillegonda J. George, Michigan.
Collection of Becky Keck, Martinez, California. Hand pieced.

Great Grandmother's Delight. 63" x 82".
1999. Becky Keck, Martinez, California.
Machine pieced by maker and commercial machine quilted by Nina Farrell at New Pieces.

Rose Wreath (detail). Unquilted top.
Martha Sawyers Simonson (1853-1937),
Willits, California. Hand appliquéd with
buttonhole stitch. Collection of
Leith Sorensen, Antelope, California.

When I stayed with Bernadette DeCuir, she showed me a lovely Rose Wreath quilt top which started a chain of events. The quilt was made by the great-grandmother of her son's mother-in-law, Martha Sawyers Simonson. The wreath, stem, and flowers were hand appliquéd with a tiny buttonhole stitch.

Bernadette was inspired to make her version of the quilt. She chose to use her sewing machine to do the appliqué, however. Bernadette used a blanket stitch to appliqué the flowers, stems, and vines and a zigzag stitch to attach the small round flower centers.

Bernadette asked her friend, P.J. Davey, to machine quilt the top on her commercial quilting machine. She used a Double Dahlia motif in the plain blocks and filled in with stipple quilting.

P.J. was so intrigued with Bernadette's quilt that she decided to make her own version. She opted to hand appliqué the blocks with tiny buttonhole stitches as Martha had done in the original. (It took her six hours to complete each block.) She added a Garden Maze border and Prairie points to her version. P.J. used a heart motif for the quilting pattern this time.

Martha's Rose Quilt. 78½" x 94½".
1999. Bernadette DeCuir,
Rocklin, California. Machine
appliquéd and pieced by maker and
machine quilted by P.J. Davey.
Project instructions begin on page 105.

Martha's Rose Quilt (II). 90" x 104".
1999. P.J. Davey, Weaverville, California.
Hand appliquéd with buttonhole stitch and machine quilted.

I instantly fell in love with a quilt owned by Gay Nichols. Her maternal grandmother, Ruth Hunter Foster, fashioned a postage stamp medallion of two-inch squares which was literally an encyclopedia of fabrics. The quilt makes us realize just how many different fabrics can be joined successfully in one quilt. The quilt inspired Gay to make her quilt, *Grandmother's Gift*.

Gay also inherited a stack of blocks that her grandmother had made. Ruth loved the floral appliqué pattern and stitched it repeatedly so there would always be a supply on hand. Gay recalls her own first quilting experience when she was ten years old: "My mother and grandmother machine stitched green sashing to join the floral blocks. I helped them make comforters, tying black perle cotton in the center of each flower's circle and in the corners of the sashing."

From the remaining stash of floral blocks, Gay selected four to be the medallion center of her own quilt. She cut finished two-inch squares from reproduction fabrics and feed sack bits-and-pieces I gave her. She even salvaged fabric from a set of antique blocks, often having to combine three pieces of fabric to make the squares large enough. Gay found making the quilt was a way to connect with her mother and grandmother. She says, "For me, making *Grandmother's Gift* was like having a conversation with the two of them."

Postage Stamp Medallion. 74" x 74".
1930s. Ruth Hunter Foster, Oregon.
Hand pieced and hand quilted (used stencils).
Collection of Gay Nichols, Albany, California.

Grandmother's Gift. 50$\frac{1}{2}$" x 50$\frac{1}{2}$".
2000. Gay Nichols, Albany, California.
Appliquéd squares from the 1930s by Ruth Hunter Foster. Machine pieced and machine and hand quilted by Gay Nichols. Project instructions begin on page 97.

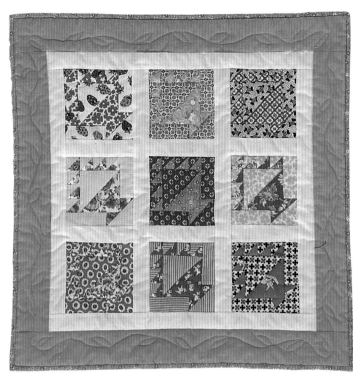

Grandma's Baskets. 25" x 25".
1998. Margaret A. Price, Moraga, California.
Machine pieced and machine quilted.

Margaret Price was trying to use up some fabric that had belonged to her mother and grandmother. She had promised her mom that she would make something with it. (Margaret says, "A little quilt goes a long way.") *Grandma's Baskets* was the result.

Margaret loves Basket blocks. Each block features a feed sack or vintage conversation print paired with a reproduction fabric. The border is made from blue chambray that Margaret used when she stitched her first garment as a teenager.

"The featured fabric in *Red Feed Sack Stars* is a bright, large-scale print that always seemed to overpower any vintage or reproduction prints I paired with it. The fabric languished in my closet just as it had in my mother's and grandmother's fabric stashes. All the while, this bright fabric wanted to star in its own quilt!" says Margaret.

Margaret combined the red feed sack with other forty-to-seventy-year-old printed fabrics from her inherited scrap bags and placed them on a muslin background. Notice the simple, fragmented star border and how it sets off the quilt center. I think Margaret's mother and grandmother would be pleased that she was finally able to figure out what to do with the red feed sack.

Red Feed Sack Stars. 55½" x 55½".
2000. Margaret A. Price,
Moraga, California. Machine pieced,
hand appliquéd, and machine quilted.

I first saw Susan Bond's work at a one-woman show at New Pieces Gallery in Berkeley. A Mariner's Compass quilt made with feed sacks caught my attention. The block was an unusual choice for feed sacks. I was intrigued. Susan says, "I became interested in feed sacks after seeing stacks and stacks of them at a quilt show a few years ago. Even though many women were hastily sifting through them, I had never heard of anyone actually using them in a quilt. The prints of the various sacks just felt so classically American that I decided I should try using them in one of America's oldest traditional art forms, the quilt."

Susan's Mariner's Compass was foundation pieced and set into a medallion format. Additional stars are pieced into the background. Susan used a white linen fabric for the background rather than muslin. The quilt is beautifully hand quilted.

After her experiment, Susan warns others about choosing patterns with sharp points and appliqué, "Many of the sacks are more loosely woven than the fabric that quilters are accustomed to using. Foundation piecing or appliqué is a must."

Sail on Sacks of Flour. 58^1/$_2$" x 70". 1998. Susan Bond, McCall, Idaho. Machine pieced, hand button hole stitched appliqué, hand quilted.

Sometimes a project starts as a phone conversation. As I described the Wagon Wheel quilts I was working on (pages 45-47) to Barbara Wilson, she told me she had a quilt her mother had made. It was a wheel shape, but the block pieced into a square shape rather than a hexagon like mine.

Barbara made a contemporary version of the quilt with plaid and stripe fabrics. I encouraged her to use the Patrick Lose hand-dyed-look fabrics for the background of the blocks. My sister, Roberta Horton, supplemented Barbara's collection of plaids and stripes with ones she had designed for Fasco/Fabric Sales. It's fun to give old blocks a new look.

Detail of *Rosia's Wagon Wheels*.
68" x 89". 1939 or 1940. Rosia A. Scott
(1905-1986), Colorado.
Hand and machine pieced and hand quilted. Collection of Jan Fairbanks, Bremerton, Washington.

New Hot Wheels. 50" x 70".
1999. Barbara J. Wilson,
Citrus Heights, California.
Machine pieced and quilted.
Collection of Roberta Horton
and Mary Mashuta.

Air Ship Propeller, II. 60" x 80".
1999. Barbara J. Wilson, Citrus Heights, California.
Machine pieced by maker and hand quilted by Dee Davis.
Collection of Jan Fairbanks, Bremerton, Washington.

When Barbara decided to replicate her mom's quilt it became a mixture of now and then. She drafted her block (#3499) on her computer using Block Base™. (This Electric Quilt Company™ program uses Barbara Brackman's Encyclopedia of Pieced Quilt Patterns.) She mail ordered feed sacks from the Kirk Collection. I wonder what her mom would have thought about all that is available to assist quilters today?

A Thing About Baskets. 38" x 42".
1990. Kathy Sward, Muir Beach, California.
Machine pieced, hand appliquéd, and hand quilted.

Kathy Sward took a Story Quilt class from me in 1989. When we shared possible stories, she was upset because she didn't feel she had a story worthy of a quilt project. She did confess that she liked basket quilts and said that she used to make baskets. She went home to think. She didn't get anywhere until she went into her workroom. There were baskets everywhere: a pieced basket pincushion, baskets stuffed with "great projects for another day," a basket of cards purchased "just because," a miniature Amish basket quilt for a teddy bear, and many pieced basket blocks and pictures.

Kathy had purchased vintage fabrics, feed sacks, and linens for twenty years at house sales and thrift stores, most of it on trips back to Kansas. She included a lot of them in *A Thing about Baskets*.

Ten years later a wonderful quilt caught my eye at a national quilt show. It was the kind of quilt I look at and say, "I wish I had made that one." Kathy had continued her collecting, and she was at it again. She had created a second basket quilt with vintage fabric. She says that creating *Playing Old Favorites: Kitchen Ragtime* made her remember "... my favorite little ruffled-edged skirt (my mother made it from a feed sack) with white and yellow daisies outlined in black. We didn't have a lot; we always made do. This quilt—in the spirit of that tradition—makes me happy. I look at it and smile." And so do I.

One of the things that is so appealing about Kathy's quilt is that she was able to take traditional blocks made with traditional fabrics and set them in a more contemporary way within skewed settings. We know it's from "now" even though it feels like it's from "then."

Playing Old Favorites: Kitchen Ragtime. 46" x 50".
1999. Kathy Sward, Muir Beach, California.
Machine pieced, hand appliquéd, and hand quilted.

Food Quilt: In My Grandmother's Kitchen. 73" x 84". 1997. Susan Dague, Piedmont, California. Machine pieced and quilted.

Susan Dague began collecting vintage fabrics, feed sacks, tablecloths, tea towels, curtains, and aprons in the mid-1980s. She searched antique stores, flea markets, thrift stores, and the vendor malls at quilt shows. (She even visited some of the same shows that I did, but I wasn't ready to "see" these treasures yet.) She also bought and traded feed sacks with mail-order vendors.

One of Susan's special areas of interest has been food fabrics. She says, "I loved them. I found the first few and just started finding more. The variety amazed me. There were soooooo many prints, and so few duplicates." As much as she loved the fabrics, they were hard to work with because most were printed on white. She decided she needed to design something with non-white spaces. The Square-in-a-Square block allowed for non-white to be used in a regular, repeating manner.

Originally the blocks were set in straight rows, but Susan experimented until she found a better set. (Polaroid™ pictures kept an accurate record as she reconfigured the block layout.) An off-set version won. It took a while to come up with the Streak of Lightning border. After it was attached, the overall design of the quilt disappeared! A red checked inner border saved the day. (Notice that the check repeats in the binding.)

Susan says of the quilt, "This quilt brings me a lot of pleasure. When shown, it brings out the most positive responses from people. Most find it very comfortable, which was my goal. This was the first quilt of mine that anyone other than my husband ever described as 'fabulous.'"

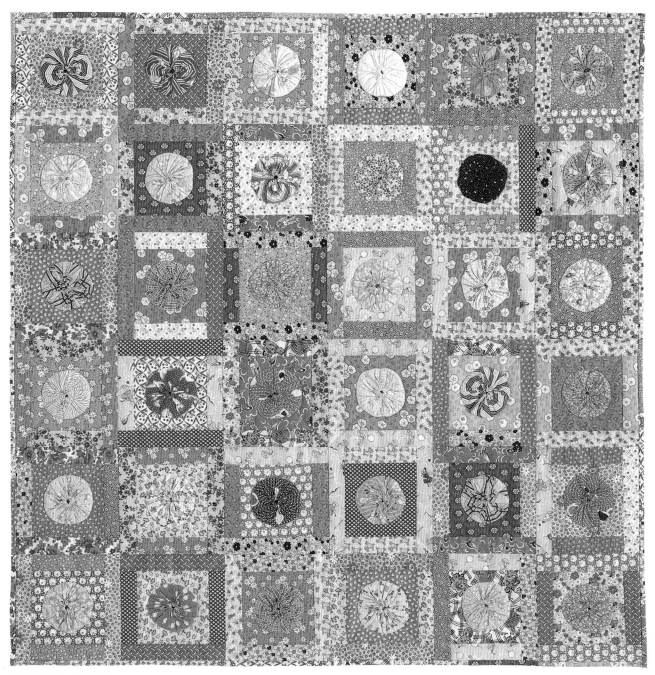

YoYo Quilt. 40" x 40". 1999.
Nancy Pagani, El Cerrito, California.
Vintage yoyos; hand appliquéd and machine quilted.
Collection of Susan Pagani, Oakland, California.

Nancy Pagani makes contemporary quilts and wearables. On a trip to Jacksonville, Oregon she found several strings of yoyos in an antique store. The giant three-inch yoyos had been rescued from a deteriorating quilt. Nancy just had to have them. Once she got them home, they languished until Nancy bought ten-inch squares of '30s reproduction fabrics. After hand appliquéing the yoyos to 4$^1/_2$" squares, she added additional 1" strips to each block in the way you would add logs when making the Courthouse Steps version of Log Cabin. The logs give the effect of sashing, but they are more irregular and playful. The pieced sashing further reinforces the original design constraint of working with ten-inch squares of fabric.

Nancy's daughter, Susan, immediately fell in love with the quilt and Nancy was pleased to give it to her.

Carroll Griffiths had a collection of '30s reproduction prints. She had been wanting to try English paper piecing but didn't want to commit to a whole quilt. A patchwork vest seemed like a perfect project because she could piece a variety of block patterns and then somehow combine them. She knew she should do the project when she found the perfect antique button necklace at a quilt show to wear with the vest. Then a friend gave her a yoyo pin made with '30s prints. Carroll found a black-and-white antique button in her button collection to use for a closure . I admire Carroll's flawless workmanship and the vest is no exception. She has done a good job of fitting the four quilt patterns into the vest pattern pieces.

'30s Vest. 1998. Carroll Griffiths, Modesto, California. Paper pieced.

Back view of '30s Vest

Using Leftovers

It's easy to get involved with the preciousness of the fabric when you are dealing with feed sacks and vintage fabrics. Once you use it, there may be no more available. The next question is, "How small of a piece of fabric should I save?" Miniatures, doll quilts, using repetitive shapes, string quilts and wearables are some possible projects that might help answer that question for you.

If you enjoy small-scale work, miniatures may be the answer for precious fabric leftovers. Even though Kathy Sward usually works full-scale, she enjoys the challenge of an occasional miniature quilt. Her *Trip Around the World* quilt has ¼" finished squares and ⅛" seams. She used small-scale vintage and reproduction fabrics. The yellow check is a feed sack. What can I say, except isn't it wonderful?

Trip Around the World. 8" x 8¼".
1997. Kathy Sward,
Muir Beach, California.
Machine pieced.

Doll quilts are always a good way to use up special extra fabric. They are easier to cut and sew than miniature quilts that are much more of a challenge. Doll quilts don't require a lot of fabric and are done fairly quickly. These were all made with vintage fabrics.

Kitty Doll Quilt. 13" x 13". Maker unknown. Hand pieced and quilted. Collection of Roberta Horton, Berkeley, California.

One-Patch Doll Quilt. 10" x 12". Maker unknown. Pieced and quilted by hand. Collection of Nancyann J. Twelker, Shoreline, Washington.

Four-Patch Doll Quilt. 11³/4" x 17¹/2". Maker unknown. Hand pieced. Collection of Roberta Horton, Berkeley, California.

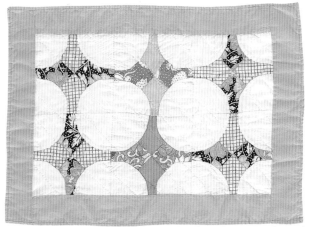

Improved Four-Patch Doll Quilt. 14³/4" x 21". Maker unknown. Hand pieced and quilted. Collection of Nancyann J. Twelker, Shoreline, Washington.

Nine-Patch with Alternating Block Doll Quilt. 15" x 18¹/2". 1990. Joyce Pennington Fleckenstein, Washington. Machine pieced and hand quilted. Collection of Nancyann J. Twelker, Shoreline, Washington.

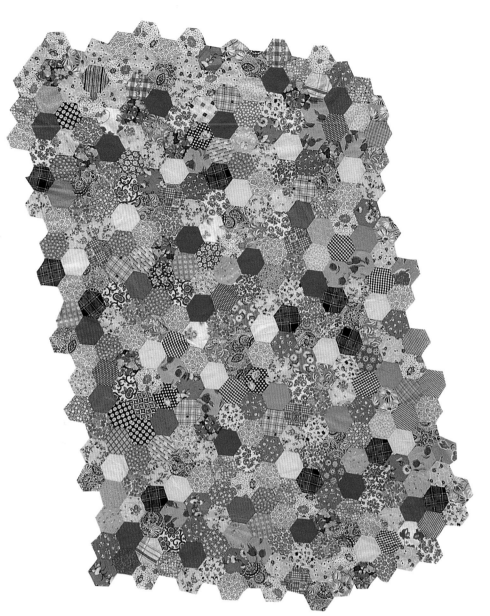

Fragment of *Giant Hexagons*. Maker unknown.
Hand pieced. Collection of Susan Dague, Piedmont, California.

Detail of *Diamond Scrap Quilt*
(quilt shown on page 14).

Snowball blocks. Mary Mashuta.

Another way to work is to pick a shape and cut it from scraps as you go along. Eventually you will have enough pieces for a quilt. This Diamond quilt is a good example of a one-shape scrap quilt.

The *Giant Hexagons* is another example of a one-shape quilt. "Giant" is the operative word. The hexagons measure $3^{1}/_{2}$" high x $4^{1}/_{2}$" on a diagonal measure. The top is obviously a "work-in-progress."

If you prefer to machine piece, I think it would be much easier to piece Snowball blocks than Hexagons. Solid triangles are needed to show off the octagon shapes.

Detail of *Missouri String Quilt*

The string quilt is another wonderful "user-upper" of extra fabric. You can even use the scraps of the scraps. Strings are saved as long as there is adequate fabric that will show after two seams are stitched. The strings are sewn over paper shapes in the stitch-and-flip method (you stitch the two pieces with right sides together, flip the pieces open, and press). Then the excess fabric is trimmed from around the edges and the paper is removed. The hardest thing for contemporary quilters to do is to make the strips random, uneven widths. We are too accustomed to strip piecing even widths of fabric cut with our rotary cutter and rulers.

The strings of *Missouri String Quilt* are sewn diagonally across squares of paper. An "X" shape emerges when four blocks are sewn together. The "X" is reinforced because common fabrics are often used in the four adjoining blocks. The blocks are sashed with a home-dyed, beige sashing and smaller string posts. The quilt contains several strings of Halloween fabric. Notice the heart motifs quilted in the sashing.

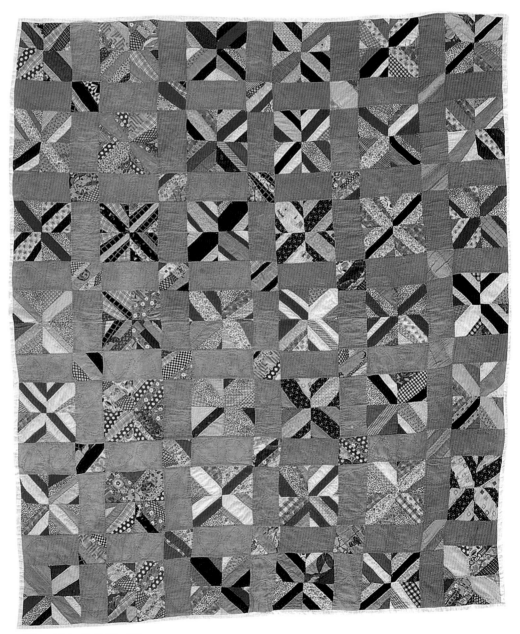

Missouri String Quilt. 72" x 87".
Maker unknown. Hand pieced and quilted.
Collection of Kathy Sward, Muir Beach, California.

Indian Hatchet String Quilt is a variation that uses the basic Indian Hatchet unit. The strings are paper pieced to the paper diagonal piece and plain triangles are added to complete the square. The blocks can be configured in many ways. Here they form "X" shapes in the middle of the quilt and a zigzag border around the edge.

Indian Hatchet String Quilt. 60" x 72". 1996.
Susan Dague, Piedmont, California.
Machine pieced and machine quilted with meander stitching.

Triangle String Quilt.
62" x 81". Maker unknown.
Machine quilted by
Susan Dague in 2000.
Collection of Susan Dague,
Piedmont, California.

Triangle String Quilt is made with large triangles. It's a perfect project for when you are really tired but would like to stitch on your machine. Even though the quilt looks very random, there are rules to follow. Each triangle needs to be stitched with at least two strings, but not more than five strings. It works best to use a variety of mis-matched fabrics selected at random rather than using strings that have been carefully co-ordinated. Be sure to evenly distribute light and dark values. Contrast works well. And lastly, work to have a variety of fabric types—prints, solids, geometrics, and linear patterns.

String quilts are fun and let us practice the old-fashioned American quality of frugality. This is a great lesson for our "throw-away" society.

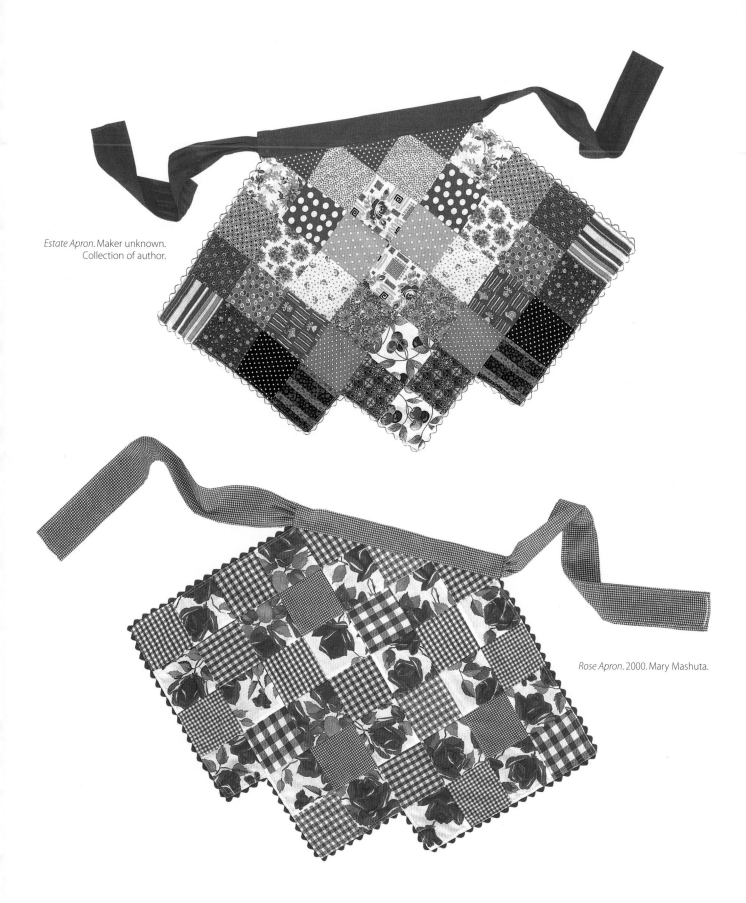

Estate Apron. Maker unknown.
Collection of author.

Rose Apron. 2000. Mary Mashuta.

Another possibility for leftovers is to make an apron from them. I found a charming one at an estate sale and decided to create my version of it with a rose feed sack that belonged to my publisher's grandmother. Since the red-and-white theme was established by roses, I added red-and-white checks from my collection.

Machine Quilting

Even though the vast majority of quilts made from 1920 to the 1970s were hand quilted, I have decided to include a chapter on machine quilting because that's what many quilters do today. Let's face it, one of the reasons that so many quilt tops have come down to us is probably that their makers never got around to hand quilting them!

hand quilting

My emphasis in this chapter will be on machine quilting, but first a few words about traditional hand quilting. Each pattern piece in a block could be outlined all the way around like Dee Davis has done in *Air Ship Propeller*. We assume the stitching was always ¼" from the seam, but often this was a "more or less" measurement. (They didn't use ¼" masking tape.)

A "faster results method" was to quilt in the Baptist Fan pattern as in *Prairie Queen*. Repeating arcs were drawn on the quilt with a pencil. A stencil or a string with a series of knots tied in it could be used to space the arcs in an individual ring. Sometimes the arcs were drawn on the plain muslin backing of a quilt, and it was quilted from the wrong side because it was easier to see the lines. (This made the marking easy to see, but let's face it, our quilting stitches look best on the side we see as we quilt.)

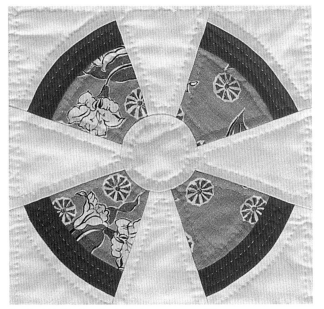

Detail of *Air Ship Propeller* (quilt shown on page 57).

Detail of *Prairie Queen* (quilt shown on page 49).

Detail of *Grandmother's Gift* (quilt shown on page 53).

machine quilting

Today many quilters have turned to the sewing machine to get the job done faster. It is permissible to combine hand and machine quilting in the same quilt. Gay Nichols straight-line machine quilted the many, many small squares in her quilt, but hand quilted in a wave pattern around her grandmother's appliqué motifs in *Grandmother's Gift*.

If you don't do the quilting yourself, you can hire it out. Traditionally church quilting bees and individuals hand quilted for a fee—often a set amount per spool of thread used. Today we have professional machine quilters who use good quality domestic machines or even commercial quilting machines. They operate out of their homes or quilt stores. In fact, more and more quilt stores offer this service. Becky Keck had Nina Ferrel at New Pieces in Berkeley free-motion machine quilted Becky's *Great Grandmother's Delight* in a simple pattern.

Detail of *Great Grandmother's Delight* (quilt shown on page 51).

Detail of Martha's Rose Quilt (quilt shown on page 52).

Free-Motion Machine Quilting

For free-motion machine quilting, the feed dogs (which normally control the flow of the fabric through the machine) are dropped. The machine operator guides the quilt through the sewing machine as the stitches are formed to create the stitched design. The idea is to keep going for as long as possible without stopping the stitching line. There are many continuous-line quilting design patterns available. The designs can be simple or very elaborate and beautiful. Some quilters have made free-motion machine quilting a fine art, but it does take patience and practice to master this technique.

P.J. Davey free-motion machine quilted Rebecca De Cuir's *Martha's Rose Quilt* with a Dahlia pattern, arcs, and stippling. She used heart wreaths, heart motifs, and stippling in her own quilt, *Martha's Rose Quilt (II)*.

Detail of Martha's Rose Quilt (II)
(quilt shown on page 52).

Straight Line Machine Quilting

I am now going to tell you how I machine quilt. Read through and see what you can adapt to how you machine quilt. I think it is easier to become proficient in straight-line machine quilting than free-motion quilting. My students feel good about their skill level after only two or three hours of actual stitching practice.

Even though my Bernina® sewing machine is capable of dropping its feed dogs, I am not physically able to do free-motion machine quilting. I don't consider it an option. If I can't do the job with straight lines, I don't do it.

Straight-line machine quilting is done with the feed dogs in the normal position. An even-feed walking foot attachment is a necessity. It makes the top and bottom of the quilt move through the machine at the same time. In regular stitching the feed dogs pull the bottom of the quilt through a little faster and drag lines result on the back of the quilt.

I use a combination of stitching-in-the-ditch next to seam lines and decorative straight stitching to machine quilt my work.

Let's begin with "nuts and bolts" information.

mary's machine quilting hints

Helpful hints for selecting equipment:

- If you have a lot of trouble machine quilting with your old machine, it may be time to upgrade to a better model. A good quality sewing machine pays off in the long run.

- For best results purchase a walking foot made specifically for your machine. (Pfaff® machines have one that is permanently attached.) It is possible to purchase generic walking feet which may or may not work for you.

- If your machine has a knee lift lever, make yourself learn to use it. You then have both hands free to reposition your work. If your machine doesn't have a knee lift, investigate purchasing a generic one.

- Make sure you have good lighting and good glasses so you can see what you're trying to do. Upgrades may be necessary.

Helpful hints for selecting supplies:

- Select a good quality batting. I prefer to work with cotton/polyester blends (Fairfield Soft Touch®, Hobb's Heirloom®, Warm & Natural™). Follow the manufacturer's instructions for preparation.

- I use rayon thread because I like the sheen. Fine quality machine quilting thread also works.

- I also use size 8 perle cotton with a size 16 needle to quilt and embellish some of my quilts. The larger size thread shows more, particularly on busy prints. Prewashed Hobbs® Heirloom batting works best.

- Monofilament thread can be used for stitching-in-the ditch where you don't want the stitches to show as much as they would with regular thread. (However, I don't recommend it for feed sacks and vintage fabrics because they are more fragile and the thread may be too strong for them.)

- I never use cotton-covered polyester thread (it builds up static electricity in your tension mechanism), cotton thread that comes on the big spools (poorer quality; okay for piecing), or embroidery thread (too weak; only three-ply).

- Buy good quality needles. I use Schmetz Jeans/Denim in size 80/12 for most tops. Fragile, thinner fabrics would stitch better with 60/10 because it makes smaller holes. Machine quilting needles may be more readily available in your area. (Don't use Universal needles. The point is too dull, so the line of stitching isn't as straight.)

- Use size 16 Top Stitching needles for heavier threads like size 8 perle cotton.

Helpful hints for constructing a top that will be machine quilted:

- Limit first projects to 60" x 60" or less, preferably MUCH less. Large quilts are a lot to handle. Why make things harder?

- Finger press as you sew blocks. Do a good job of pressing with an iron on the steam setting when the block is complete.

- Make sure the back looks as good as the front. Seams pressed the wrong direction make your job harder later on because they will not lie flat.

- Think about how you will quilt the top as you construct and press it.

- I press seams to one side if I plan to stitch-in-the-ditch. For an all-over design such as Baptist Fan, some people prefer to press the seams open. It gives a flatter surface to stitch on.

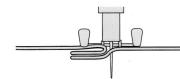

Stitch-in-the-ditch in the valley or side with only one layer of fabric.

Seam pressed open.

Back detail of *Check Wagon Wheel* (quilt shown on page 46). Press seams to one side when you plan to stitch-in-the-ditch.

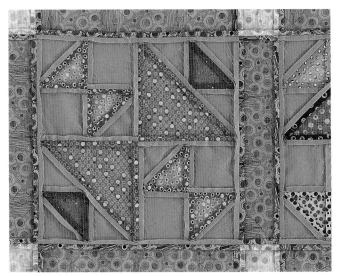

Back detail of *Not So Many Dots* (quilt shown on page 20). Press seams open when you plan to quilt an all-over design such as Baptist Fan.

If the completed top has many seams at the edge, machine baste around the top ⅛" from the edge to secure seams before you layer it with batting. This also helps to keep the fabric from raveling back too far. Some feed sacks are very loosely woven and tend to ravel.

Touch-up press the top before it is basted, if necessary.

Helpful hints for basting:

1. Tape the backing to a table or floor with small pieces of tape, wrong side up, before laying the batting on it. (It needs to be smooth, but not taut.) Then add the batting and the top, right side up.

2. Use a large ruler to help you align rows so they are straight. If the quilt is crooked when you baste it, how can you expect it to be straight after it is quilted?

3. Use good quality safety pins. The $1^1/_8$" size are easiest to use. Large safety pins fill up too much space and get in the way; small pins are hard to open and close.

4. Safety-pin baste with your pins placed about a fist's-width apart. Try not to place pins too near seams or over them. You may start anywhere. It's not necessary to baste from the center out as you do in thread basting.

5. Remove the tape. Pin the outer edges of the quilt with straight pins placed perpendicular to the edge. Hand baste close to $^1/_8$" machine basting. Remove the straight pins.

6. Trim excess batting and backing to $^1/_2$" at edge. Longer edges tend to get caught underneath the quilt as you shift it around. It's so easy to inadvertently catch them in your stitching.

Helpful hints for better stitching while straight-line machine quilting:

- A slow-to-moderate, even sewing machine speed produces the best results. (Some machines have a half speed.)

- If your stitching line weaves back and forth, slow down. Sewing more slowly helps you to be more accurate.

- The LONGER your stitch length, the EASIER the quilt will move through the machine. On my Bernina I lengthen it to somewhere between $3^1/_2$ to 4 which is 8-10 stitches per inch. (This also shows off pretty threads more.)

- Remember to always reset your machine to the longer stitch length when you turn it on.

- Always pull the bobbin thread up before you begin stitching. This prevents thread snarls on the bottom side. Hold both threads when you begin stitching.

- Figure out a secure, but non-showy way to secure your stopping and starting so that you don't have to tediously bring the ends to the back, tie them off, and work them in. (You will have to do this with heavier threads or where stops and starts would really be obvious, as in stitching a circle design.)

- Some machines will stitch in place two or three stitches as a securing stitch, but this isn't strong enough for machine quilting. If your machine will zigzag a very small stitch with a width less than .5 mm, try this for about $^1/_{16}$"; otherwise stitch with very small stitches for $^1/_8$"-$^1/_4$" and then immediately switch to the longer stitch length.

- Always test your anchoring stitch by tugging on the thread ends to see if you can pull it out easily.

- When you pivot or make slight adjustments on curves, make sure your needle is in the down position. Lift the presser foot, leave the sewing machine needle down, turn the quilt, then lower the presser foot. Some machines have a needle-down position.

- Take only one stitch after you pivot. Sometimes the needle doesn't go down where you think it will after you turn. You can always remove the last stitch and reposition it, but if you have stitched two stitches it is too late.

- Remember to take frequent breaks and stretches. Set a timer, if necessary.

start machine quilting

Now it is time to get to the actual quilting. I begin by doing stitching-in-the-ditch quilting. These are lines of stitching that are done to anchor the seams in a quilt. The stitching is utilitarian, not pretty.

Stitching-in-the-ditch is done close to, but not on top of, a seam line. The seam has been pressed to one side. The resulting high side, or hill, has three layers of fabric. The low side, or valley, has only one.

Stitching-in-the-ditch is done in the valley because it is less noticeable. If you stitch on the side that has all the seams, the stitching will show more because they act like padding.

For example, with a sixteen-block quilt the blocks would be anchored in place by the time all the basic rows of vertical and horizontal stitching has been done close to the edges of the blocks. To begin, roll the quilt vertically and stitch the middle seam from top to bottom. (As you approach intersections, look carefully ahead of where you are stitching, the hill and valley may switch on the other side.) Unroll the quilt and re-roll it horizontally. Stitch the middle row from side to side. Complete the stitching between the rows.

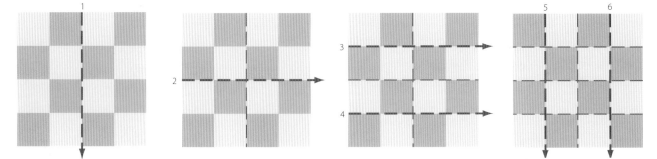

Order of stitching-in-the ditch. Lines 1 and 2 are the basic anchor; lines 3, 4, 5, 6 complete the basic grid.

Now that you have stitched the basic grid, unroll the quilt and just pull up a block at a time to work on. In our example, the quilt is made up of Eight-Pointed Stars. Each block has been secured around the edge, but now the seams within the block must also be stitched. There will be two rows of vertical stitching and two rows of horizontal stitching. Since I stitch-in-the-ditch EVERY TIME there is a seam, the "kitty ears" will also have to be stitched.

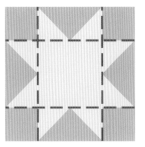

Stitch-in-the-ditch both vertically and horizontally.

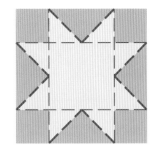

Also stitch the "kitty ears." (You won't be able to rotate the quilt, so each set of "ears" will have to be done separately.)

Stitching-in-the-ditch is monotonous and boring to do, but it really helps you to have a flat quilt. (As you stitch, you can be thinking about the pretty stitching you will add when you have finished the boring part.)

Adding Stitching That Shows

Once the stitching-in-the-ditch is completed, the fun begins. Since all the block pieces are anchored at their seams, it isn't necessary to stitch ¹/₄" around each of them. In fact, it can't be done easily. So, instead, we concentrate on adding pretty stitching that will show.

Let's see what can be done with our basic Eight-Pointed Star. There are a number of possibilities to consider when adding stitching to the triangles. All are based on the structure of the triangle. They reinforce what is already there. Remember that each beginning and end will have to be secured, and that some of the possibilities will involve pivoting.

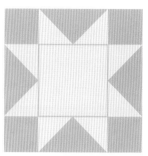

Eight-Pointed Star

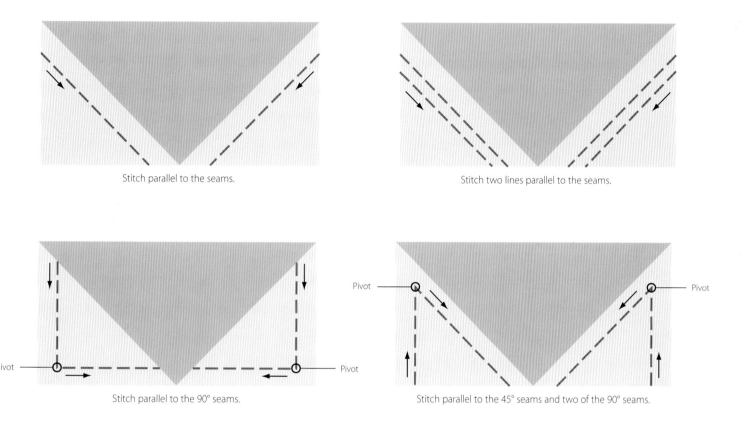

Stitch parallel to the seams.

Stitch two lines parallel to the seams.

Stitch parallel to the 90° seams.

Stitch parallel to the 45° seams and two of the 90° seams.

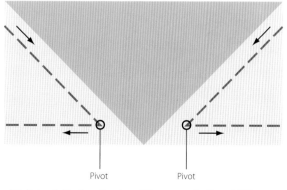

Stitch parallel to the other two 45° seams and adjacent 90° seams.

Now let's consider the square in the middle of the block. Look at the basic structure. Corners and mid-points present possibilities beyond basic lines. Mirroring a structural line with a second line of stitching makes it much more visually interesting.

I mark the basic lines with tape. It is easily removed, unlike chalk and pencil. I often use the edge of my walking foot as a measurement guide for second lines of stitching.

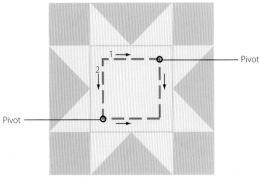

Stitch parallel to the seams.

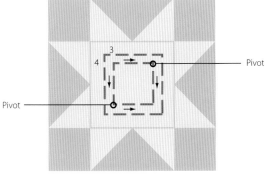

Stitch two lines parallel to the seams.

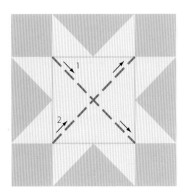

Stitch two lines diagonally from corner to corner.

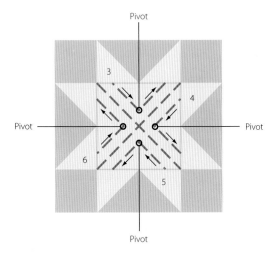

Stitch two lines diagonally from corner to corner, then stitch parallel to the first stitching.

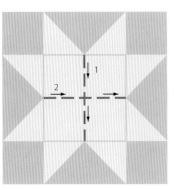

Stitch horizontally and vertically.

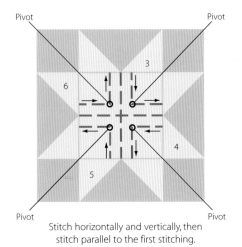

Stitch horizontally and vertically, then stitch parallel to the first stitching.

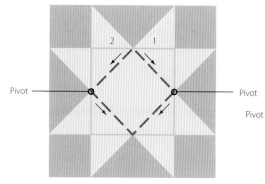

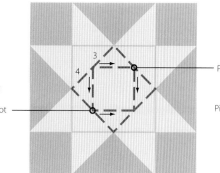

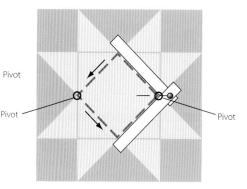

Stitch from the mid-point of one seam to the mid-point of the next seam for all four seams.

Stitch from the mid-point of one seam to the mid-point of the next seam for all four seams, then repeat, stitching from the mid-points of the first stitching.

I used $3/4$" tape to temporarily mark the line from mid-point to mid-point. A pin marks the pivot point.

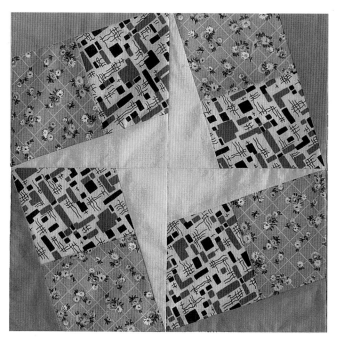

Detail of *Fiesta Stars*, unquilted top

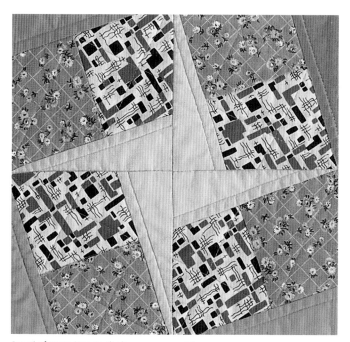

Detail of *Fiesta Stars* (quilt shown on page 34).

Looking at the Structure

Let's look at the straight-line machine quilting used in quilts from the book.

Compare the two photos above. The unquilted block comes alive with the addition of quilting lines that reinforce the basic structure of the block. The star points get one line of stitching. I used the edge of the walking foot as my measuring device.

You may want to take the time to add additional stitching to the star center. (I found the creases from folding the quilt were less apparent when I did this, but it is a lot more work.)

Detail of *Red Check Stars* (quilt shown on page 35).

Stitching Outside the Lines

To speed the decorative stitching, I have learned to stitch across the lines of piecing and get the job done sooner, rather that only stitching within each block section. Most of the time, I still stitch-in-the-ditch first. The Diagonal Cross and Nine-Patch blocks required four lines of decorative stitching each. The lines were marked with masking tape. The lines were placed ³/₄" from the edges of the cross and the nine-patch pieces. An additional "X" marked the nine-patch center.

Detail of *Plaid Diagonal Cross and Nine-Patch* (quilt shown on page 32).

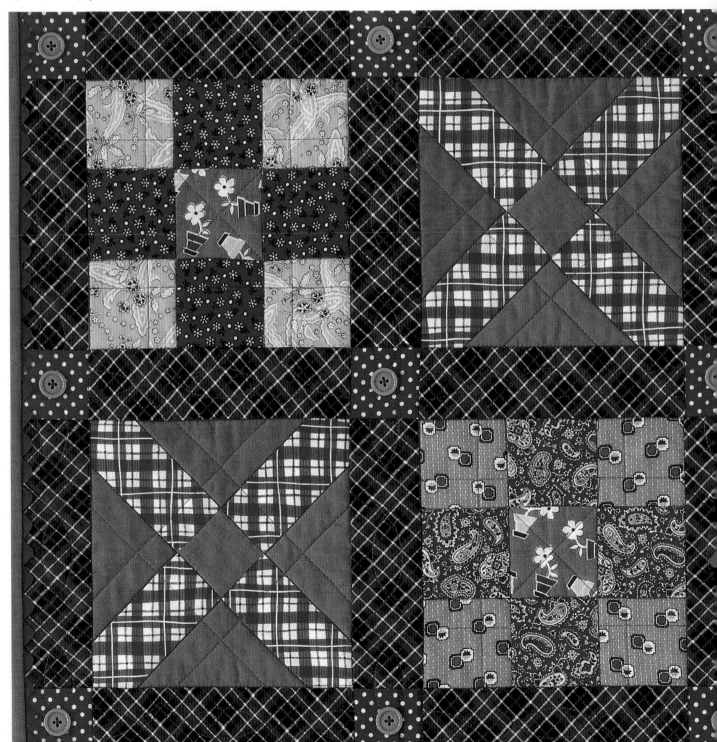

Creating a Grid

All-over grids are fast to quilt because there is a minimum of stopping and starting. Susan Dague created an all-over diagonal plaid quilting design to reinforce the plaid posts in *Blue Check Sashed Squares*. Notice that some of the lines are double stitched for variety. She used ¼" tape to ensure that her lines would remain evenly spaced.

Sometimes it is possible to superimpose a grid over the quilt that is based on the quilt block pattern. This worked for me in *Peach Nine-Patch*. Since I knew I was going to do some kind of overall design, I pressed the seams open as I constructed the top and didn't do my usual stitching-in-the-ditch.

I stitched rows of vertical and horizontal lines through the centers of the nine-patches first. This created a basic, square pattern of lines. Then I stitched two smaller squares in each section of the grid, using ¾" masking tape as a width guide.

Next I stitched a square-on-point for variety. To top things off, I added a stitched circle to each square. To ensure a perfect circle, I stitched around a freezer paper circle. (Because there was nowhere to hide the beginning and ending of my stitching, I brought all the threads to the back, tied them off, and worked in the ends.)

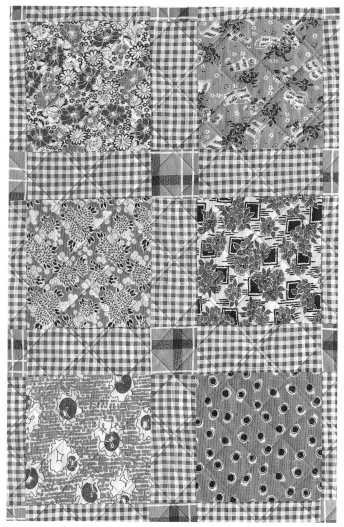

Detail of *Blue Check Sashed Squares* (quilt shown on page 23).

Detail of *Peach Nine-Patch* (quilt shown on page 27).

Stencils

Commercial stencils are a source of quilting patterns. They can be used in a variety of ways. Usually the lines are transferred with a pencil or chalk. I have even used stencils to cut freezer paper designs.

A commercial stencil of a delicate cable was the perfect size and design to reinforce the illusion of light zigzags that Susan created in her quilt. The cable was used to connect the white, background print triangles.

The Baptist Fan quilting design can also be transferred from a stencil. I have had trouble getting the marking completely removed when I have used a lead pencil, silver pencil, or chalk. (I use an eraser for pencil lines and a natural bristle nail-scrub brush for chalk lines.) Now I only mark the first (largest) and last (smallest) arcs and eyeball the distance between the arcs. (Some walking feet have a small bar attachment which lets you evenly "mirror" previous stitching lines.)

Detail of *Food Quilt*:
In My Grandmother's Kitchen
(quilt shown on page 60).

Freezer Paper

I learned I could transfer the shapes to be quilted without marking on my quilt. At first I cut the shapes out of paper and pinned them in place. I always had to be careful of the pins so they wouldn't stick me! But then I switched from computer paper to freezer paper because it was stronger. Eventually it dawned on me that I could press the freezer paper in place with a warm iron and not have to use pins!

After a shape is cut and pressed into place with a warm iron, you then stitch next to the paper. A freezer paper pattern piece can be used over and over, just make sure you always have the shiny side down when you press.

When I stitched the circles in *Peach Nine-Patch* (page 27), I worked on one circle at a time. The same was true for the flower motifs used in *Plaid Posy Patch* (page 32), *Nebraska Giant Four-Patch* (page 25), *Seventies Nine-Patch* (page 28), and *Out-of-Sight Circles* (page 44).

Continuous designs like cables require more freezer paper pieces. If you are using a cable, trace and cut enough shapes to fill one whole length of border or one row of vertical or horizontal sashing. Stitch a continuous line between the shapes of the cable design. Eyeball the distance between motifs.

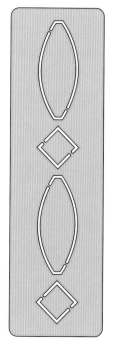

Use a stencil to trace and cut out the shapes from freezer paper.

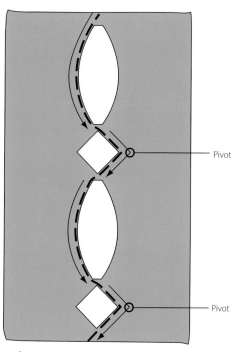

Pivot

Pivot

Iron freezer paper shapes onto the quilt top and stitch a continuous line between the shapes to create the cable design.

Detail of *Green Nine-Patch* and *Snowball* (quilt shown on page 30).

Circle Within Circle blocks were also enhanced with freezer paper stitching. I used size 8 perle cotton (with a size 16 top stitching needle). For *Out of Sight Circles* I cut swags from freezer paper for the wedges of the circles and petal flowers for the inner circles. I used Baptist fan arcs to create the shapes between the circles that fill the background. Since it is background space, I stitched with rayon thread in an aqua color.

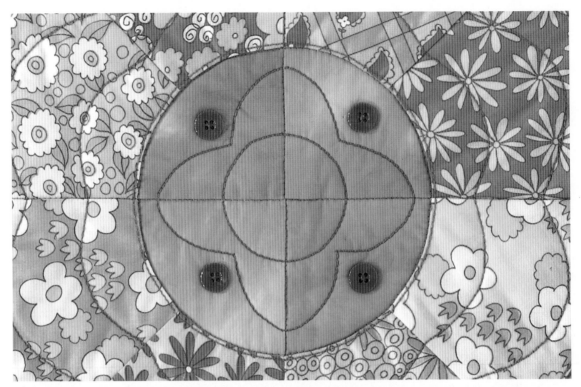

Detail of *Out-of-Sight Circles* (quilt shown on page 44).

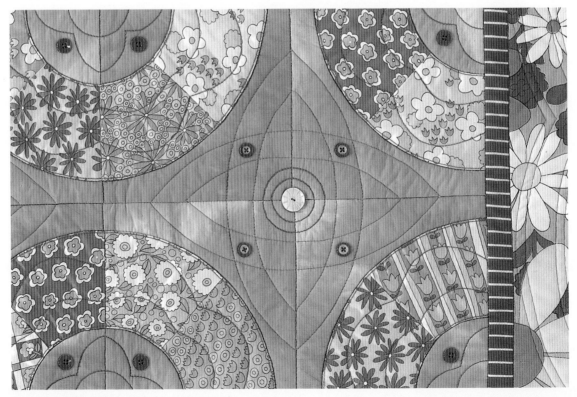

Detail of *Out-of-Sight Circles* (quilt shown on page 44).

For my inner border cables on *Fiesta Stars* (page 34) I cut my long ovals and pressed them into place to begin my stitching. The length of the ovals was based on the combined length of two squares in the adjoining pieced border. Additional lines were added after I had stitched from oval to oval.

I cut my scalloped pieces for the border of *Fiesta Stars*. (Again, the measurement was based on the length of the same two squares.) The pieces were evenly spaced, pressed into place, and one line of stitching was done. Then it was simple to mirror the shapes as I stitched additional rows. I used the edge of the walking foot as my guide.

Detail of *Fiesta Stars* (quilt shown on page 34).

Back detail of *Circle Within Circle*
(quilt shown on page 42).

Since I had been unhappy with the markings left on my quilts when I used a Baptist Fan stencil, I decided to try the freezer paper idea. I traced the beginning and ending Baptist Fan arcs, cut them out, and pressed them onto the quilt. I used the stencil as a guide while I placed the arcs.

In Conclusion

Remember that there are many steps in making a quilt. Quilting is one of the last, but it should be as important as selecting the pattern and fabrics. Good quilting breathes life into your quilt; poor quilting detracts from your work. I continually challenge myself to try different approaches to my machine quilting and keep discovering new patterns and techniques I can try with straight-line stitching. Each quilt is a new opportunity to grow. There are many ways to cover the surface with lines; I just keep in mind that I want to have an even amount of quilting across the quilt surface. Sometimes this is only evident on the back of the quilt!

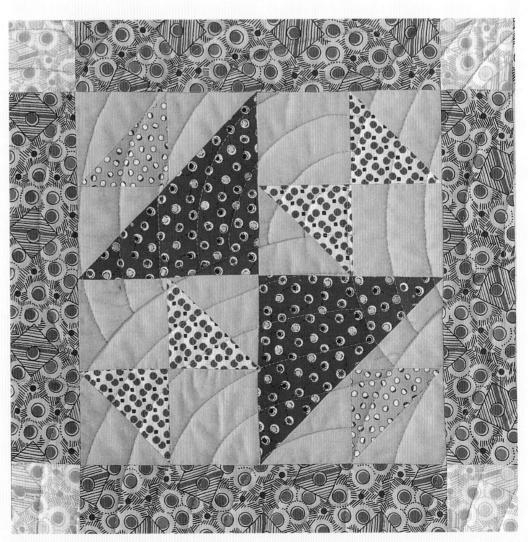

Detail of *Not So Many Dots* (quilt shown on page 20).

PROJECT:
Circle Within Circle

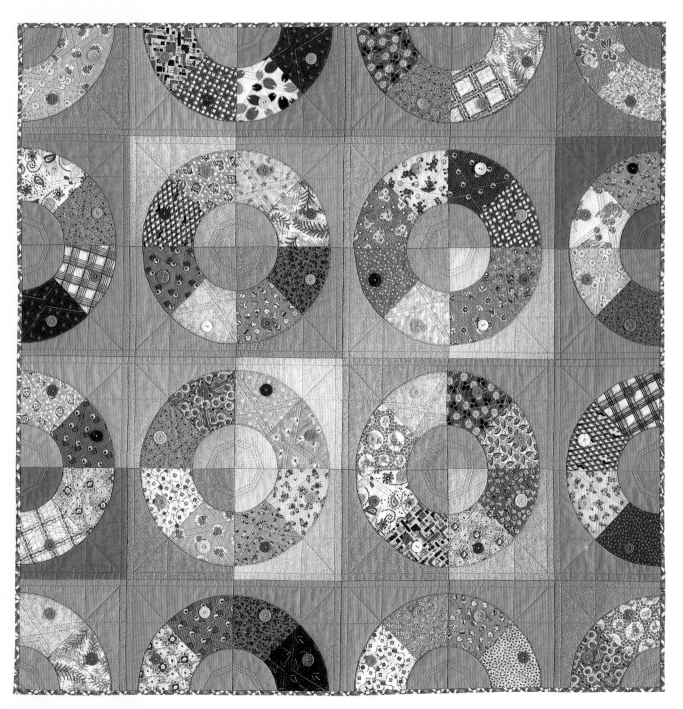

Circle Within Circle. 45¹/₂" x 45¹/₂". 1999. Mary Mashuta. Machine pieced and appliquéd. Machine quilted with rayon and perle cotton threads. Embellished with vintage buttons.

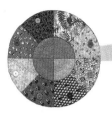

Materials

(Fabric requirements are based on a 42" fabric width.)

Circles
- 72 squares 6" x 6" of print scraps

Background
- 36 squares 8" x 8" of solid or solid-like print scraps

Backing

50" x 50"

Binding
- 1/2 yard of print or solid

Batting

50" x 50"

Template plastic

72 buttons

Size 8 perle cotton thread

Cutting

Blocks
- Cut 72 arcs from prints using template A.
- Cut 36 squares 8" x 8" from background fabric.

Binding
- Cut 5 strips 2" x 42" from print. Sew into one long strip.

Block Construction

(1/4" seam allowance)

1. Lay out all of the cut pieces referring to the quilt photo. Rearrange the pieces, if necessary, to obtain enough contrast between the circle pieces and the background squares.

2. Stitch the A pieces together to form four circles, eight half-circles, and four quarter-circles. To

fold the edges under, machine baste 1/4" from the curved edges. Clip the seam allowances of the inner circles. Fold the curved edges under and press. Pin or baste in place.

Quilt Construction

1. Sew the background squares into rows. Press Row 1 seams to the left, Row 2 seams to the right, etc., so the seams nest when the rows are sewn together.

2. Sew Rows 2 and 3 together. Press. Sew Rows 4 and 5 together. Press.

3. Place the circles and partial circles onto the background, matching the horizontal and vertical seams of the circles to the horizontal and vertical seams of the

background squares, referring to the quilt photograph. Pin or baste in place.

4. Machine stitch using a straight stitch 1/8" from the inner and outer circle edges using regular thread or perle cotton.

5. Sew the rows together to complete the quilt top.

Finishing

1. Layer, baste, and quilt. Perle cotton thread may be used instead of regular thread if you want the quilting to show more.

2. Sew the buttons on, referring to the quilt photograph.

3. Press the binding in half lengthwise and sew onto the quilt using your preferred method.

A

grain

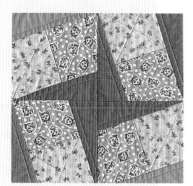

PROJECT:
Fiesta Stars

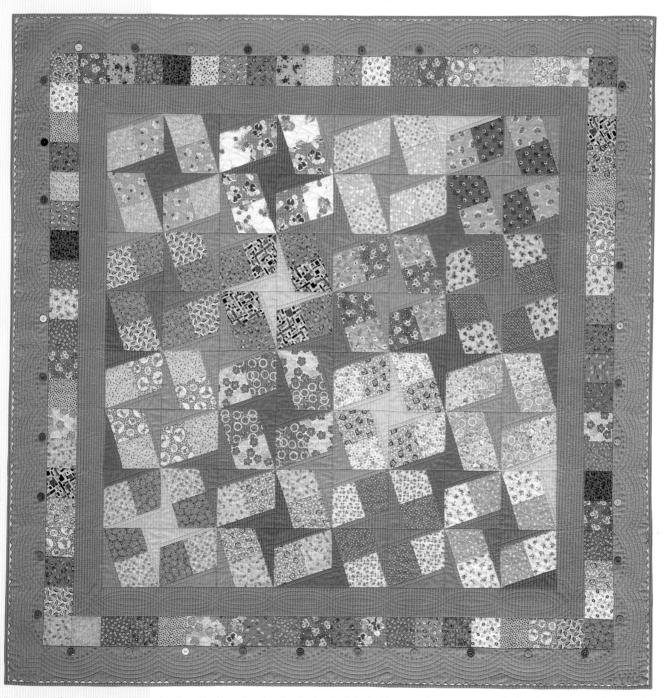

Fiesta Stars. 66¹/₂" x 66¹/₂". 1999. Mary Mashuta. Machine pieced and quilted; embellished with vintage buttons, variegated rick rack, and variegated sashiko thread.

Materials

(Fabric requirements are based on a 42" fabric width.)

Stars

Note: fat quarters may be used

- ¹/₄ yard of yellow solid
- ¹/₄ yard of aqua solid
- ¹/₄ yard of blue solid
- ¹/₄ yard of bubblegum pink solid
- ¹/₄ yard of lavender solid
- ¹/₄ yard of green solid
- ¹/₄ yard of peach solid

Background

- ¹/₄ yard each of thirty-two different prints (coordinate sixteen sets; one medium and one light print)

Inner Border

- ³/₄ yard of peach solid

Pieced Border

- 76 squares 3¹/₂" x 3¹/₂" from scraps or leftover background yardage

Outer Border

- 1 yard of aqua solid

Backing

71" x 71"

Binding

- ³/₄ yard of peach solid

Batting

71" x 71"

Template plastic

- 7¹/₂ yards of ⁵/₈" rick rack (four packages of Wrights® Jumbo Printed Rick Rack)
- 40 buttons
- Variegated sashiko thread or size 8 perle cotton thread

Cutting

Stars (Use Template A)

- Cut 16 from yellow solid.
- Cut 23 from aqua solid.
- Cut 22 from blue solid.
- Cut 15 from bubblegum pink solid.
- Cut 20 from lavender solid.
- Cut 20 from green solid.
- Cut 12 from peach solid.

Background (Use Template B)

- Cut 4 from each print.

Note: *If you stack cut the pieces, each layer of fabric must be right-side up or some of your cut pieces will be backward.*

Inner Border

- Cut 5 strips 3¹/₂" x 42" from peach solid. Sew into one long strip. From this:
- Cut 2 strips 3¹/₂" x 48¹/₂" for the top and bottom.
- Cut 2 strips 3¹/₂" x 54¹/₂" for the sides.

Pieced Border

- Cut 76 squares 3¹/₂" x 3¹/₂" from scraps or leftover background fabric.

Outer Border

- Cut 7 strips 3¹/₂" x fabric width from aqua solid. Sew into one long strip. From this:
- Cut 2 strips 3¹/₂" x 60¹/₂" for the top and bottom.
- Cut 2 strips 3¹/₂" x 66¹/₂" for the sides.

Binding

- Cut 7 strips 2¹/₂" x fabric width from peach solid. Sew into one long strip.

Block Construction

(¹/₄" seam allowance)

1. Lay out all of the cut Star block pieces referring to the photo on page 89.

2. Each block will make one quarter of the star.

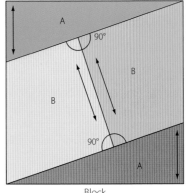

Block

3. Pick up the first two B pieces, place them right sides together matching the dots, and stitch along the side with the 90° corners (B Unit). Press.

4. Place an A piece onto the B Unit with right sides together matching the dots and stitch following the diagram above. Press. Repeat for the other A piece. Place this block back into the quilt layout.

Note: *You may find it helpful to use a sandpaper board to carry the unfinished blocks to the sewing machine. The sandpaper keeps the fabric in place when transporting it from the design area.*

5. Repeat to make 64 blocks. Unfinished blocks should measure 6¹/₂" x 6¹/₂".

Quilt Construction

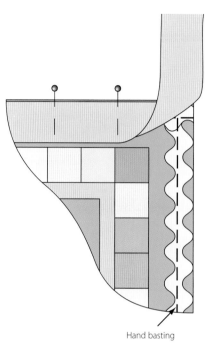

Hand basting

Hand baste rick rack to quilt, then stitch binding. Trim.

Quilt Construction

1. Sew the blocks into rows. Press Row 1 seams to the left, Row 2 seams to the right, etc., so the seams will nest when the rows are sewn together.

2. Sew the rows together. Press.

3. Sew on the inner border strips; first the top and bottom, then the sides. Press.

4. Sew 18 of the $3^1/2$" border squares together. Press. Repeat. Sew onto the top and bottom edges of the quilt top. Press.

5. Sew 20 of the $3^1/2$" border squares together. Press. Repeat. Sew onto the sides of the quilt top. Press.

6. Sew on the outer border strips; first the top and bottom, then the sides. Press.

Finishing

1. Layer, baste, and quilt. Machine or hand stitched sashiko or perle cotton threads may be used for some of the rows of quilting.

2. Sew the buttons on, referring to the quilt photograph.

3. Hand baste the rick rack to the edges of the quilt matching the edges of the rick rack with the edges of the quilt.

4. Fold the binding strip in half lengthwise and press.

5. Stitch the binding to the edge of the quilt using slightly wider than a $1/4$" seam allowance. The stitching should follow along the concave curves of the rick rack.

Note: *You may find it helpful to punch a 1/16"*
hole to mark the dot on each template.

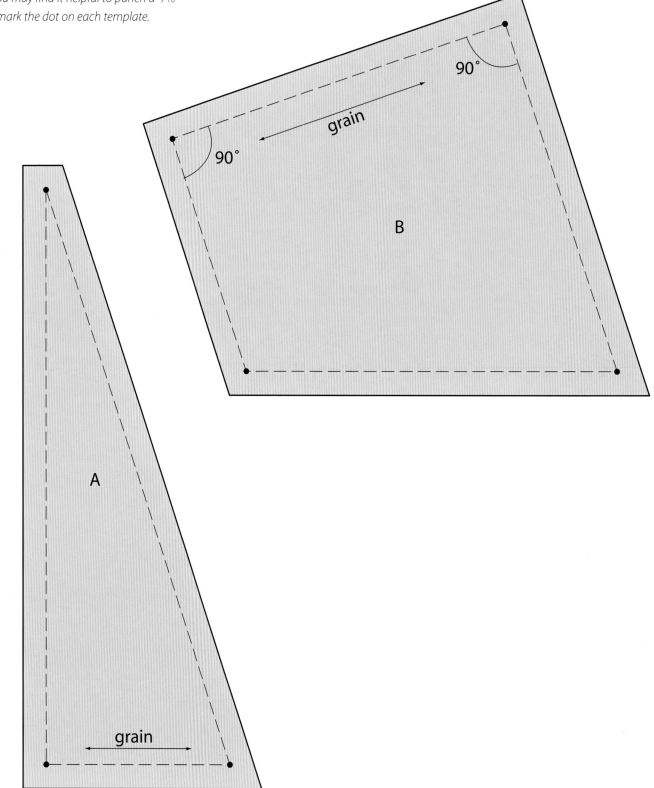

PROJECT:
Check Wagon Wheel

Check Wagon Wheel. 38" x 36 ¹/₂". 2000. Mary Mashuta. Machine pieced, appliquéd, and quilted.

Materials

(Fabric requirements are based on a 42" fabric width.)

Wagon Spokes

- Print scraps at least 3¹/₂" x 5" for a total of 2 yards

Center Circles

- Solid scraps at least 3" x 3" for a total of ³/₈ yard

Background

- Checked scraps at least 5" x 3¹/₂" for a total of 2 yards or ¹/₄ yard each of five different checks.

Backing

- 42" x 41"

Binding

- ³/₈ yard

Batting

- 42" x 41"

Template plastic

Light-weight cardboard

Cutting

(¹/₄" seam allowance included on all templates)

Wagon Spokes

Option 1: From a variety of prints, cut 126 using Template B, cut 10 using Template E and 8 using Template E-Reverse.
OR
Option 2: You may wish to coordinate the spokes in each "wheel" with fabrics in the same color family. If this is the case, there are:

- 16 complete wheels; each requiring 6 pieces cut from Template B.

- 2 quarter-wheels; each requiring 1 piece cut from Template B and 1 piece cut from Template E.

- 8 half-wheels (X); each requiring 2 pieces cut from Template B and 1 piece cut from Template E and 1 piece cut from Template E-Reverse.

- 4 half-wheels (Y); each requiring 3 pieces cut from Template B.

Center Circles

- Cut 30 from solids using Template A.

To prepare circles:

1. Cut a circle from light-weight cardboard using the dashed line of Template A.

2. Hand baste ¹/₈" from the edge of the fabric circle.

3. Place cardboard template on the circle and pull the basting threads taut.

4. Press the edges in place to make a perfect circle.

Background

Option 1: Cut 130 using Template C, 6 using Template D, and 4 using Template D-Reverse.
OR
Option 2: As with the wagon spokes, you may wish to coordinate the backgrounds of each wheel. If this is the case, there are:

- 16 complete wheels; each requiring 6 pieces cut from Template C.

- 2 quarter-wheels; each requiring 1 piece cut from Template C and 1 piece cut from Template D.

- 8 half-wheels (X); each requiring 3 pieces cut from Template C.

- 4 half-wheels (Y); each requiring 2 pieces cut from Template C and 1 piece cut from Template D and 1 piece cut from Template D-Reverse.

Binding

- Cut 4 strips 2 x 42". Sew into one long strip.

Block Construction

(¹/₄" seam allowance throughout. Press all seams to the same side so they radiate around the hexagon.)

1. Alternating 6 background pieces cut from Template C and 6 print pieces cut from Template B, sew the long sides together.

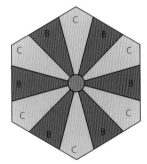

Complete Wagon Wheel Block

2. Appliqué one solid circle to the center of each block.

3. Make 16 complete wheels. Unfinished wheel should measure 8³/₄" from one flat side to another.

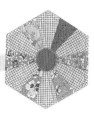

4. Make 2 quarter-Wagon Wheel blocks, 8 half-Wagon Wheel (X) blocks, and 4 half-Wagon Wheel (Y) blocks in the same manner following the illustrations.

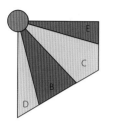

Quarter-Wagon Wheel Block

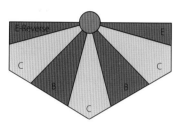

Half-Wagon Wheel Block (X)

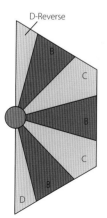

Half-Wagon Wheel Block (Y)

5. Appliqué one solid circle to the center of each half and quarter block. The circle will be trimmed to size after you have completed piecing your top.

Quilt Construction

1. Lay out the blocks in a pleasing arrangement.

2. Matching spoke to spoke, pin and sew blocks together from point of one C to the point of the next C, starting and stopping ¹/₄" away from beginning and ending of each seam. Backstitch at each end.

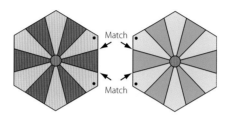

Sew together starting and stopping at the marked dots.

3. Make 2 rows with one quarter-wheel and 4 half-wheels (X).

4. Make 4 rows with 4 complete wheels and 1 half-wheel (Y).

5. Starting and stopping ¹/₄" away from the beginning and ending of each seam, sew the rows together matching the points on C. Backstitch at each end. Press.

6. Lay quilt top flat and trim the edges of the circles on the outer edges of the quilt top even with the pieces on either side of them.

Finishing

1. Layer, baste, and quilt as desired.

2. Press binding in half lengthwise and sew onto the quilt using your preferred method.

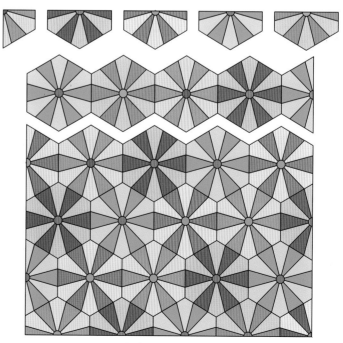

Quilt Top Construction

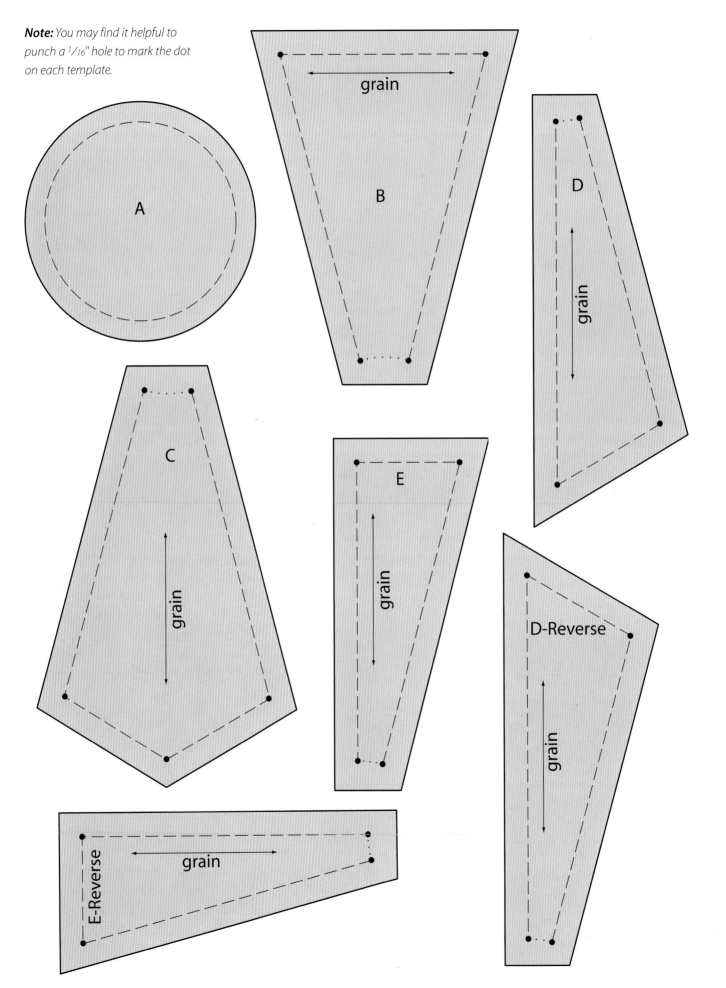

Note: *You may find it helpful to punch a ¹/₁₆" hole to mark the dot on each template.*

A

B

grain

D

grain

C

grain

E

grain

D-Reverse

grain

E-Reverse

grain

PROJECT:
Grandmother's Gift

Grandmother's Gift. 50¹/₂" x 50¹/₂". 2000. Gay Nichols, Albany, California. Appliquéd blocks from the 1930s by Ruth Hunter Foster. Machine pieced and machine and hand quilted by Gay Nichols.

Materials

(Fabric requirements are based on a 42" fabric width.)

Flower Blocks

- 12 squares 5" x 5" of print scraps for the flowers
- 12 rectangles 3$^1/_2$" x 4$^1/_2$" of green scraps for the leaves
- $^3/_8$ yard of off-white for block backgrounds

Background and Outer Border

- 505 squares 2$^1/_2$" x 2$^1/_2$" from print scraps or $^1/_8$ yard each of 35 different prints

Inner Border

- $^3/_8$ yard of yellow print

Backing

55" x 55"

Binding

- $^1/_2$ yard of print or scraps

Batting

55" x 55"

Black embroidery floss

Light-weight cardboard

Template plastic

Cutting

Flower Blocks

- Cut 12 from print scraps using Template A.
- Cut 12 from green scraps using Template B.
- Cut 4 squares 11" x 11" from off-white.

Background and Outer Border

- Cut 505 squares 2$^1/_2$" x 2$^1/_2$" from prints.

Inner Border

- Cut 2 strips 1$^3/_4$" x 42" for the sides.
- Cut 2 strips 1$^3/_4$" x 42$^1/_2$" for the top and bottom.

Binding

- Cut 5 strips 2" x 42" from print or 2$^1/_2$"-wide strips from scraps. Sew into one long strip.

Block Construction

(1/4" seam allowance)

1. Refer to the instructions on page 94 to turn under the exposed edges of the flowers. Turn under a scant $^1/_4$" on all exposed edges of the leaves. Press. Baste if desired.
2. Position the flowers and leaves on the off-white squares referring to the quilt photo.
3. Hand stitch with black embroidery floss, using a running stitch.
4. Trim the blocks to 10$^1/_2$" x 10$^1/_2$".

Quilt Construction

Quilt Top

1. Position the stitched blocks referring to the quilt photo.
2. Stitch 5 of the 2$^1/_2$" squares together. Press. Attach this sashing to one edge of one flower block. Press. Attach a second flower block to this sashing. Press. Repeat for the other 2 flower blocks.
3. Stitch 11 of the 2$^1/_2$" squares together. Press. Stitch this sashing to one set of flower blocks. Press. Stitch the set of blocks to this sashing. Press.

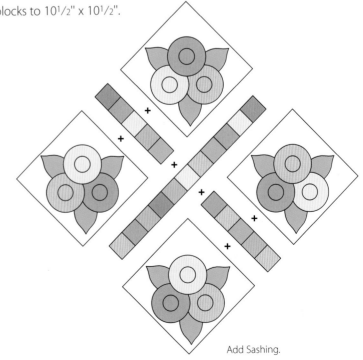

Add Sashing.

4. To construct Unit 1, stitch eleven 2½" squares together in a row. Press. Repeat three more times. You will have four rows of 11 squares.

5. Sew nine 2½"squares in a row. Press. Continue making similar rows of 7 squares, 5 squares, and 3 squares (one row each).

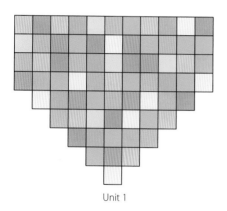

Unit 1

6. Sew these rows together adding one square as the last row.

7. Repeat to make a second Unit 1.

8. To construct Unit 2, stitch seventeen 2½" squares together in a row. Press. Continue making similar rows of 15, 13, 11, 9, 7, 5, and 3 squares.

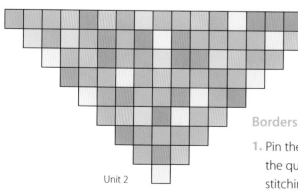

Unit 2

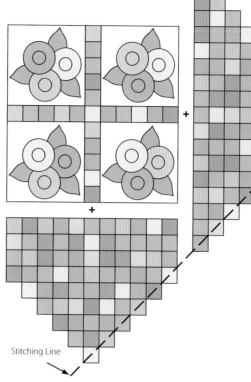

Quilt Construction

+

Stitching Line

9. Sew these rows together adding one square as the last row.

10. Repeat to make a second Unit 2.

11. Attach the #1 Units to the center block. Press.

12. Attach the #2 Units to the center block. Press.

Borders

1. Pin the inner side borders onto the quilt top matching the stitching line of Units 1 and 2 with the stitching line ¼" from the raw edge of the inner border strip.

2. Stitch the inner side borders onto the quilt top.
   Hint: Stitch with the pieced top on top and use the block intersections as a guide for placement of your stitching line.

3. Trim the quilt top even with the edge of the border strip.

4. Repeat for the top and bottom inner borders.

5. Stitch two rows of twenty-one 2½" squares together. Press. Repeat for the side outer border.

6. Attach to the sides of the quilt top.

7. Stitch two rows of twenty-five 2½" squares together for the top border. Press. Repeat for the bottom border.

8. Attach to the top and bottom edges of the quilt top. Press.

Finishing

1. Layer, baste, and quilt.

2. Press the binding in half lengthwise and sew onto the quilt using your preferred method.

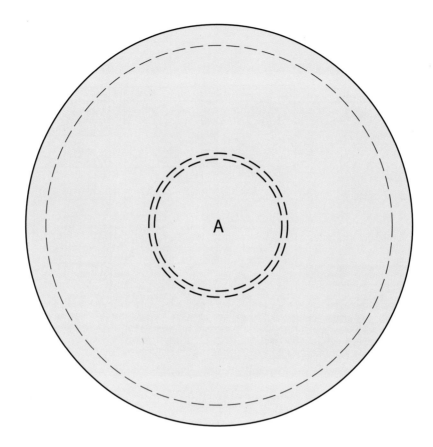

A

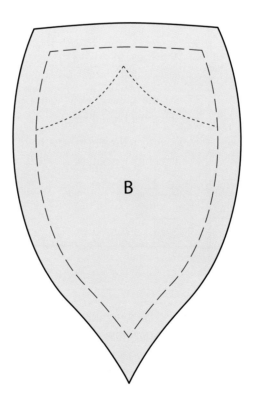

B

PROJECT:
Rainbow Baskets

Rainbow Baskets. 34 1/2" x 34 1/2". 2000. Susan Dague, Piedmont, California. Machine pieced, hand and machine quilted.

Materials

(Fabric requirements are based on a 42" fabric width.)

Baskets

- 65 rectangles 3¹/₂" x 4¹/₂" of print scraps or ¹/₈ yard of at least 20 different print fabrics (you will have leftovers) for the baskets
- 13 rectangles 6" x 8" of solid scraps or ¹/₈ yard of 13 different solid fabrics for the basket handles and bases

Background

- 1¹/₂ yards of peach solid

Backing

38" x 38"

Binding

- ³/₈ yard of pink

Batting

38" x 38"

Template plastic

Cutting

Baskets

- Cut 65 from prints using Template A.
- Cut 13 from solid for handles using Template B.
- Cut 13 from solid for handles using Template C.
- Cut 13 from solid for bases using Template D.

Background

- Cut 2 squares 6¹/₂" x 6¹/₂" from peach solid, then cut in half diagonally for the corner triangles.

- Cut 2 squares 12¹/₂" x 12¹/₂" from peach solid, then cut in half diagonally twice for the side triangles.
- Cut 13 from peach solid using Template E.
- Cut 13 from peach solid using Template F.
- Cut 13 from peach solid using Template G.
- Cut 13 from peach solid using Template H.

Binding

Cut 4 strips 2¹/₂" x 42" from pink.

Block Construction

(¹/₄" seam allowance)

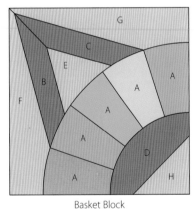

Basket Block

1. Stitch together 5 A pieces to form an arc.
2. Stitch B to F and C to G stopping at the marked dots. Backstitch.
3. Stitch B to the left side of E, and C to the right side of E stopping at the marked dots. Backstitch. Stitch the Y-seam to join F/B and G/C. Backstitch.

4. Stitch the A arc to F/B/E/C/G.
5. Stitch D to the A arc.
6. Add H. The unfinished block should measure 8¹/₂".
7. Repeat to complete 13 blocks.

Quilt Construction

1. Sew the blocks into diagonal rows. Press Row 1 seams to the left, Row 2 seams to the right, etc., so the seams nest when the rows are sewn together.
2. Sew the rows together. Press.

Finishing

1. Layer, baste, and quilt.
2. Press the binding in half lengthwise and sew onto the quilt using your preferred method.

Quilt Construction

Note: *You may find it helpful to punch a $1/16$" hole to mark the dot on each template.*

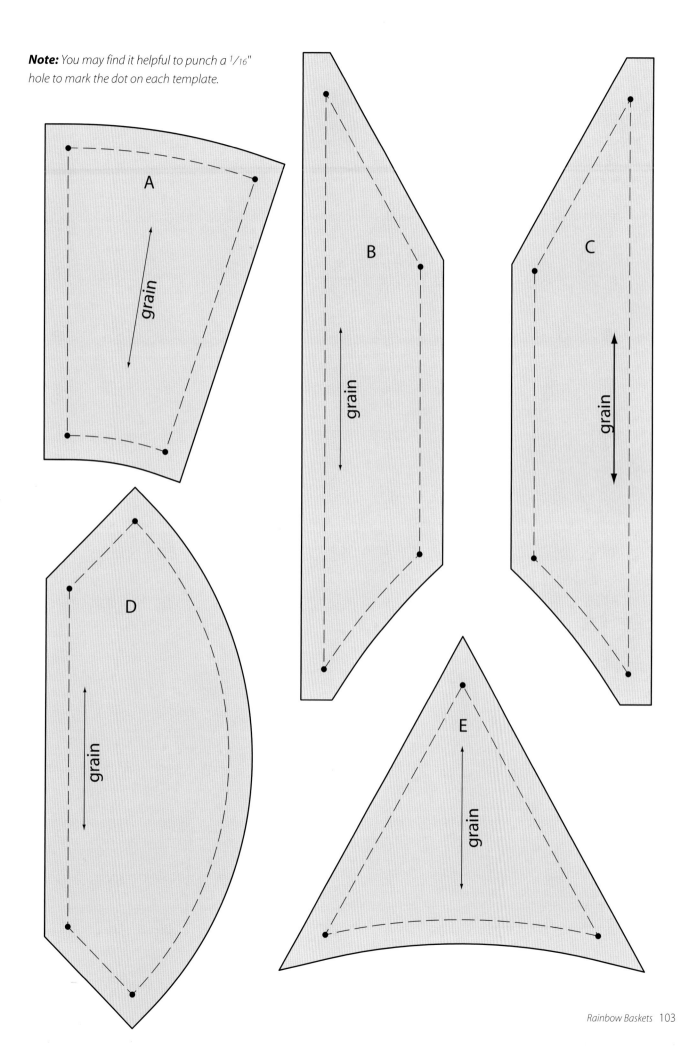

A

grain

B

grain

C

grain

D

grain

E

grain

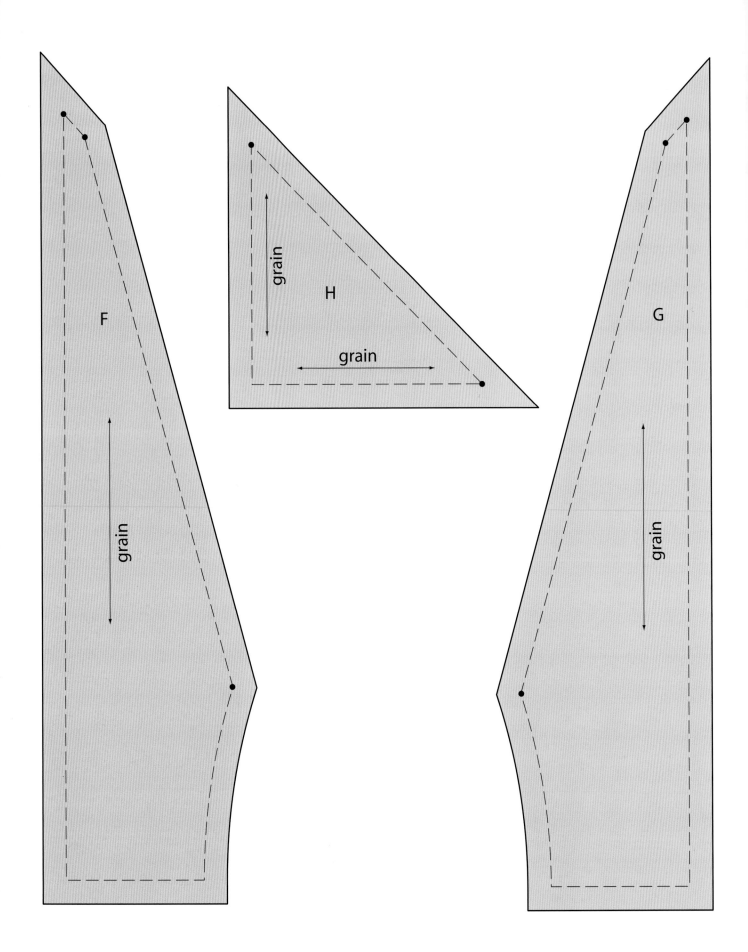

F

H

grain

grain

G

grain

grain

grain

PROJECT:
Martha's Rose Quilt

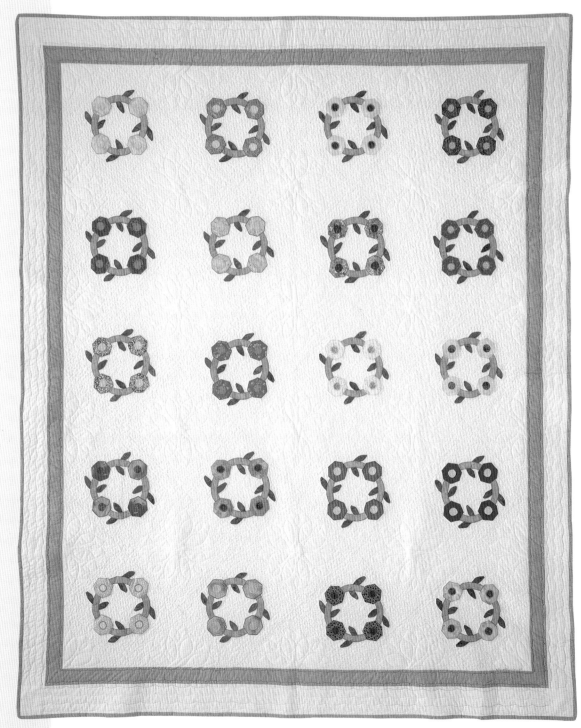

Martha's Rose Quilt. 78¹/₂" x 94¹/₂". 1999. Machine appliquéd and machine pieced by Bernadette DeCuir. Machine quilted by P. J. Davey.

Materials

(Fabric requirements are based on a 42" fabric width.)

Background (blocks, alternate blocks, setting triangles, and outer border)

- 6¹/₂ yards of off-white solid

Wreaths, Inner Border, and Binding

- 2³/₄ yards of light green texture print

Roses

- 20 scraps 3¹/₂" x 14" (one print per wreath)

Rose Centers

- 2" diameter print scraps or 20 scraps 2" x 8"

Leaves

- ³/₄ yard of dark green texture print

Backing

84" x 99"

Batting

84" x 99"

Template plastic

Lightweight cardboard

Cutting

(¹/₄" seam allowance is included on all templates.)

Off-white Background

- Cut 4 strips 12" x 42", then cut into 12 squares, 12" x 12", for the alternate blocks.
- Cut 7 strips 13" x 42", then cut 20 squares, 13" x 13", for the appliqué blocks. (These squares will be trimmed after the appliqué is complete.)

- Cut 2 squares, 9" x 9", then cut in half diagonally for the corner triangles.
- Cut 2 strips 17¹/₂" x 42", then cut 4 squares, 17¹/₂" x 17¹/₂", then cut in half diagonally twice for the side triangles (you will have 2 extra).

Wreaths

- Cut 80 from light green using Template A.

Roses

- Cut 4 from each of the twenty prints using Template B.

Rose Centers

- Cut 4 from each of the twenty prints using Template C.

Leaves

- Cut 160 from dark green using Template D.

Green Inner Border

- Cut 8 strips 3" wide across the width of the fabric. Sew into one long strip. From this cut:
- Cut 2 strips 3" x 70¹/₂" for the top and bottom borders.
- Cut 2 strips 3" x 81¹/₂" for the sides.

Off-white Outer Border

- Cut 9 strips 4¹/₂" wide across the width of the fabric. Sew into one long strip. From this cut:
- Cut 2 strips 4¹/₂" x 78¹/₂" for the top and bottom borders.
- Cut 2 strips 4¹/₂" x 86¹/₂" for the sides.

Binding

- Cut 9 strips across the width of the fabric, 2¹/₂" wide. Sew into one long strip.

Appliqué Blocks

1. Fold 13" squares into quarters and finger press. Refold into quarters on the diagonal and finger press again.

2. Using the pressed creases as guides, arrange the appliqué pieces and pin in place.

3. Prepare the center circles following the instructions on page 94.

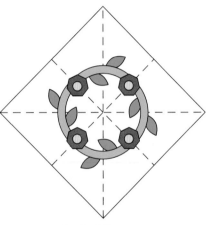

Appliqué Placement

4. Appliqué the wreath using the method of your choice.

5. Trim the block to 12" x 12".

Quilt Construction

(¹/₄" seam allowance)

1. Arrange the blocks referring to the illustration and the quilt photo.

2. Sew the blocks into diagonal rows. Press Row 1 seams to the left, Row 2 seams to the right, etc., so the seams nest when the rows are sewn together.